SECRETS
OF THE
ZODIAC

SECRETS
OF THE
ZODIAC

MICHELE FINEY

inspired LIVING

ALLEN&UNWIN

This edition published in 2010

First published in 2009

Inspired Living, an imprint of
Allen & Unwin
83 Alexander Street
Crows Nest NSW 2065
Australia
Phone: (61 2) 8425 0100
Fax: (61 2) 9906 2218
Email: info@allenandunwin.com
Web: www.allenandunwin.com

Cataloguing-in-Publication details are available
from the National Library of Australia
www.librariesaustralia.nla.gov.au

ISBN 978 1 74237 404 8

Text design by Nada Backovic
Set in 10.5/14 pt Esperanto by Bookhouse, Sydney
Printed in Australia by McPherson's Printing Group

10 9 8 7 6 5 4 3 2

For Anne

*And in memory of my fantastic Piscean grandfather,
George Finey, who spawned my interest in human
nature and inspired me to go fishing in the
cosmic ocean.*

CONTENTS

ACKNOWLEDGEMENTS

I particularly want to thank Maggie Hamilton for her encouragement and support and especially for taking the time to read my first clunky draft.

I also wish to acknowledge the contribution made by the many astrologers from whom I have learned so much; those whose books I have read, whose lectures I have attended, and for the inspiring conversations we have shared.

There are many other people to thank. Since some have chosen to remain anonymous, and I could easily overlook someone, I've thought it best not to name names.

To the many friends and colleagues who gave feedback, offered suggestions, shared their stories, gave technical help and provided much-needed moral support, I want you to know I could not have done this without you. Your help has been invaluable and I am deeply grateful.

FOREWORD

It's a common misconception that astrology is only about Sun signs and predicting the future.

Obviously, one-twelfth of the population is not going to meet the love of their life next Tuesday; nor can we be divided neatly into twelve groups, each with the same personalities and life experiences.

Sun signs and predictive astrology are only two stars in a whole universe of astrological knowledge.

The other thing you need to know is that the idea that the planets and stars somehow override our free-will is a myth; if anything, the reverse is true.

Most of today's professional astrologers are in the business of trying to help their clients develop more self-awareness so they can exercise more free-will and be less subject to 'fate'.

A horoscope is a map that symbolically describes a specific moment in time. That moment might correspond with the birth of a person, an idea, or a nation, or any other occasion. Each birth chart is unique, just as every individual is unique.

While your birth chart can tell you a great deal about your potential, what you actually do with this potential to a large extent depends on your conscious awareness and soul's development, which is an ongoing process. It's up to each of us to make the most of our talents while also learning to deal with life's challenges.

If you are new to astrology, or have only ever thought of astrology as being about predicting the future, or Sun signs, I hope *Secrets of the Zodiac* will deepen your interest in this fascinating subject.

The general principle behind *Secrets of the Zodiac* is the idea that we evolve and grow as we journey through the zodiac. The signs of the zodiac are a metaphor for the various stages of life and learning.

By exploring the natural order of the zodiac signs from Aries through to Pisces we can learn more about the basic differences that exist between people, which can lead us towards deeper self-knowledge and awareness.

Adjacent signs have a different polarity, element and quality and though they have nothing in common, we are more attuned to the earlier sign, because we have already been through that stage of development, while the sign following our Sun sign can be a real blind spot.

But since this is the direction in which we are heading, and they are right next to one another, when we encounter the sign following our Sun sign we have a real opportunity to broaden our understanding.

The serious astrologer might also wish to use this system to explore the meaning of oriental and occidental planets. Oriental planets, those that rise before the Sun, are considered pre-conscious, for we are awake to them, while occidental planets that rise after the Sun are those we are more likely to struggle to understand and integrate.

While the sign before our Sun sign is familiar to us, the sign after our Sun sign, planets in that sign and the ruling planet of that sign, can tell us something about our shadow; the aspects of ourselves we disown but which we encounter time after time so that we grow.

Michele Finey 2008

Note: All references to the seasons spring, summer, autumn or winter are based on the northern hemisphere.

INTRODUCTION

People have always watched and recorded the movements of the Sun, Moon and planets across the heavens to better understand the universe and their place within it.

As far as anyone can tell, astrology first began in Mesopotamia at least 4000 years ago.[1] Since that time astrology has spread to all parts of the world and different astrological systems have developed independently in locations as far apart as Mexico and China.

Astrology is an art, a science and a branch of philosophy all rolled into one, which is probably why it has survived to this day and continues to fascinate us.

The chief difference between astronomy and astrology is that astronomers are primarily interested in the science part, whereas astrologers perceive everything as being interconnected and that by learning how the universe operates, we can learn something about ourselves. We are a part of the universe, not apart from it. This is summed up in the astrological axiom, as above; so below.

Over recent decades, astrology in the west has become more psychologically oriented, adopting many of the ideas of psychologist Carl Jung, such as his concept of synchronicity, which is another way of explaining the mysterious connections linking the heavens to life on Earth.

Time is the dimension in which we live, so the position of the planets at a specific moment captures all the potential, opportunities and challenges of that moment which are revealed in a map of the heavens, the birth chart.

But the birth chart is not static, and nor are we. As we journey through life our awareness grows; likewise, astrologers study planetary cycles and how they correlate to stages of life and the development of the individual.

In a wider context these cycles can also help us better understand human evolution through the ages.

THE ZODIAC JOURNEY— JUST FOLLOW THE SIGNS

'Everything that irritates us about others can lead us to an understanding of ourselves.'

C.G. JUNG

Astrology is about much more than making predictions, it's about our personal development. There is an underlying principle behind the practice of astrology which is the idea that we consciously evolve as we journey through the zodiac.

The sequential order of the signs of the zodiac symbolises the various stages in this process.[2]

It's said that Aries is like a newborn child, Pisces the wise old sage, and the other signs of the zodiac represent the many stages of life and learning in between.

This means the sign that comes before our Sun sign is familiar to us, because we have already journeyed there, while our actual Sun sign represents our current developmental stage, and the next sign in the zodiac represents experiences and lessons that are presently unknown to us.

The sign which follows our Sun sign symbolises the next step in our development, for it's the direction we are ultimately heading.

There is no way to tell if we incarnate sequentially through the zodiac, and this is not the point in any case.

Just as our past is the foundation of our present, and our present actions determine our future, each sign of the zodiac contains within it the cumulative wisdom of the previous sign(s).

While the zodiac symbolises both our soul's journey in this life and over many lifetimes, this does not mean that people born with the Sun in Pisces are necessarily more evolved than everyone else. Though many Pisceans are highly spiritual people, some are not. Likewise you don't have to be born a Pisces to be spiritual. Each soul is unique, and at different stages of the journey towards wholeness.

That's why every Libran is not more 'evolved' than every Virgo, nor every Virgo more evolved than every Leo, and so on. The zodiac is a spiral. We travel around and around many times, just as the planets orbit the Sun and the Sun orbits the galactic centre.

There's no way to tell how evolved a person is by knowing their Sun sign or even by looking at their whole birth chart, because our awareness is always growing.

Yet by following the signs of the zodiac in their natural sequence, we can see that each sign has something special to teach the preceding sign and important lessons to learn from the sign that follows.

In fact, people born under the sign following our own are actually sympathetic to our situation and want us to benefit from their knowledge and experience. At the same time we often want to help those who are born under the sign that precedes our own.

Adjacent signs are always of a different element, quality and polarity and while we have virtually nothing in common with either the preceding or the following sign, it's often much easier to relate to the sign before our own than the one after, because there is a greater sense of understanding. They don't tend to push our buttons as much.

Once we understand the gifts the next sign has to offer us, we can learn to appreciate that they can teach us a great deal.

THE SUN—SYMBOL OF CONSCIOUSNESS

'...the only equivalent of the universe
within is the universe without...'

C.G. JUNG

Psychologist Carl Jung once said that only here on Earth, where opposites clash, can the level of consciousness be raised.[3]

Astrologically, the Sun represents our conscious awareness, so it's the qualities of our Sun sign we strive to develop the most.

There are many other planets and asteroids in the zodiac, and each represents an aspect of our psyche, but we identify most closely with the qualities of our Sun sign. It's at the centre of our being, just as the Sun is the centre of the solar system.

Consciousness, however, has some limitations. We can only be aware of a certain amount of information at any given time and we cannot force consciousness to grow. Our awareness continues to develop throughout life as we meet life's challenges, and many of these challenges are associated with the sign which follows our Sun sign.

Because we tend to identify so much with our Sun sign, we can become convinced that our reality is the only reality. This can result in a tendency to avoid the unfamiliar and become critical of those who are different, often resulting in unnecessary conflict.

We do this not realising we are attracting unfamiliar people and circumstances in order to help us grow. The more we resist these experiences, the more we keep repeating the same old patterns.

The art of astrology can help us appreciate that other points of view can be just as valid as our own, raise our awareness and minimise potential conflict.

THE SIGNS OF THE ZODIAC

Each sign of the zodiac is a unique combination of polarity, quality and element. These are the key components which determine the characteristics of each zodiac sign.

Sign	Polarity	Quality	Element
Aries	Yang/Extrovert	Cardinal	Fire
Taurus	Yin/Introvert	Fixed	Earth
Gemini	Yang/Extrovert	Mutable	Air
Cancer	Yin/Introvert	Cardinal	Water
Leo	Yang/Extrovert	Fixed	Fire
Virgo	Yin/Introvert	Mutable	Earth
Libra	Yang/Extrovert	Cardinal	Air
Scorpio	Yin/Introvert	Fixed	Water
Sagittarius	Yang/Extrovert	Mutable	Fire
Capricorn	Yin/Introvert	Cardinal	Earth
Aquarius	Yang/Extrovert	Fixed	Air
Pisces	Yin/Introvert	Mutable	Water

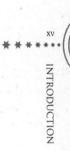

Polarity

The signs of the zodiac can be divided into various categories. The first and most basic division is into opposites. Different terms are used to describe these pairings, such as masculine/feminine and positive/negative, but these words can have other meanings, so they are not used so much today.

Yang and yin, or extrovert and introvert, are probably better ways to describe these opposing energies.

Fire and air signs are yang and are naturally extroverted; while earth and water signs are yin and more introverted.

Yang signs are: Aries, Gemini, Leo, Libra, Sagittarius and Aquarius. These signs are naturally compatible with each other.

Yin signs are: Taurus, Cancer, Virgo, Scorpio, Capricorn and Pisces. These signs also get along well together.

Signs of opposite polarity are essentially quite different from one another. Consequently, relationships between these signs are more challenging.

Quality

The zodiac is also composed of three qualities: cardinal, fixed and mutable.

These qualities are connected to the seasons. The Sun moves into cardinal signs at the commencement of each season, at the solstices and equinoxes. It moves into the fixed signs at the height of each season, when the weather is at its most intense, and then enters mutable signs when the seasons are changing and the weather is variable.

Cardinal signs, which signal the start of each season, make good leaders. They like to take the initiative and are good at making commitments, but they're not so good at following through, often because they overcommit themselves. Fixed signs are good at following through. They are persistent and determined, but not so good at adapting to change. Mutable signs manage change very well because they are adaptable and flexible, but they are not so good at taking the lead, or making a firm commitment.

Signs of the same quality are incompatible.

Cardinal signs can teach mutable signs how to make commitments. Fixed signs can teach cardinal signs how to follow through. Mutable signs can teach fixed signs how to adapt to change.

Cardinal signs (Aries, Cancer, Libra, Capricorn) are:

- *Strong-willed*
- *Natural leaders*
- *Dynamic*
- *Initiators*
- *Motivated*
- *Enterprising*

Fixed signs (Taurus, Leo, Scorpio, Aquarius) are:

- *Determined*
- *Thorough*
- *Persistent*
- *Consistent*
- *Intense*
- *Loyal*

Mutable signs (Gemini, Virgo, Sagittarius, Pisces) are:

- *Changeable*
- *Adaptable*
- *Restless*
- *Flexible*
- *Versatile*
- *Amenable*

The elements

Apart from the polarity and the quality, the zodiac is divided into four elements: fire, earth, air and water. Signs of the same element are compatible and share the same polarity.

Fire signs (Aries, Leo, Sagittarius) are:

- *Fiery*
- *Passionate*
- *Creative*
- *Courageous*
- *Enthusiastic*
- *Dynamic*

Earth signs (Taurus, Virgo, Capricorn) are:

- *Disciplined*
- *Practical*
- *Reliable*
- *Conservative*
- *Sensual*
- *Grounded*

Air signs (Gemini, Libra, Aquarius) are:

- *Intellectual*
- *Idealistic*
- *Sociable*
- *Friendly*
- *Communicative*
- *Humane*

Water signs (Cancer, Scorpio, Pisces) are:

- *Sensitive*
- *Emotional*
- *Compassionate*
- *Caring*
- *Deep*
- *Imaginative*

The elements are the gateway to understanding personality. You can identify them easily, once you know what to look for.

For example, in *Sex in the City*, Samantha is the fiery one, passionate, outgoing and spontaneous. Charlotte is the earthy one, conservative, practical and security conscious. Miranda is airy, matter-of-fact and career-minded; and Carrie is like the water element, she reflects on the nature of relationships and is looking for an emotional connection.

Similarly, in *The Wizard of Oz*, Dorothy is caught up inside a tornado and is transported to a strange land. Here she meets a host of unusual characters. Above all she wants to go home. She is seeking the security and stability of the earth element. Along the way she meets the Scarecrow who wants a brain, so he represents the air element. Then Dorothy meets the Tin Man who is looking for a heart, he wants to feel emotion, so he represents the water element; and lastly she meets the cowardly Lion who is seeking the courage of fire.

These characters are archetypal which is why they are memorable. We can easily identify with them.

Earth signs want fire signs to be more disciplined, conservative and practical.
Air signs want earth signs to be more sociable, friendly and outgoing.
Water signs want air signs to be more sensitive, compassionate and caring.
Fire signs want water signs to be more confident, assertive and active.

Astrology's greatest gift is that it can help us understand human behaviour, both our own and others', and this leads to personal growth and self-acceptance.

To reach our full potential and appreciate the value of others and what they can teach us, all we have to do is follow the natural sequence of the signs of the zodiac, just like Dorothy and her friends followed the yellow brick road.

THE RELATIONSHIP BETWEEN THE ELEMENTS

Element	Fire	Earth	Air	Water
FIRE	Similar and therefore compatible, but not conducive to growth.	Conflict, but Earth is sympathetic to Fire.	Compatible, harmonious and complementary.	Conflict. Water avoids Fire but can learn from Fire.
EARTH	Conflict. Fire avoids Earth, but can learn from Earth.	Similar and therefore compatible, but not conducive to growth.	Conflict, but Air is sympathetic to Earth.	Compatible, harmonious and complementary.
AIR	Compatible, harmonious and complementary.	Conflict. Earth avoids Air but can learn from Air.	Similar and therefore compatible, but not conducive to growth.	Conflict, but Water is sympathetic to Air.
WATER	Conflict, but Fire is sympathetic to Water.	Compatible, harmonious and complementary.	Conflict. Air avoids Water but can learn from Water.	Similar and therefore compatible, but not conducive to growth.

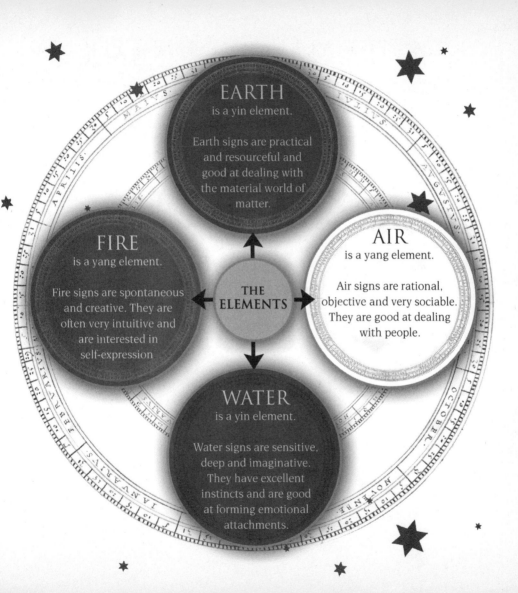

EARTH
is a yin element.

Earth signs are practical and resourceful and good at dealing with the material world of matter.

AIR
is a yang element.

Air signs are rational, objective and very sociable. They are good at dealing with people.

FIRE
is a yang element.

Fire signs are spontaneous and creative. They are often very intuitive and are interested in self-expression

THE ELEMENTS

WATER
is a yin element.

Water signs are sensitive, deep and imaginative. They have excellent instincts and are good at forming emotional attachments.

ARIES

21 MARCH–20 APRIL

'Honesty is the first chapter of the book of wisdom.'

ARIES, THOMAS JEFFERSON

YOUR LIFE MISSION

To inspire others with your courage and lead them on the journey ahead.

Your mission as an Aries is fairly straightforward; you're a hero on a quest. You thrive on a challenge and love nothing more than fighting dragons and rescuing damsels in distress. Male or female, you're the zodiac's knight in shining armour.

When people first meet you, they know straightaway you're a force to be reckoned with. You meet life head on.

Excitement and adventure are your middle names. You relish competition and pit yourself against all comers. Aries is the most honest, brave and enthusiastic sign of the zodiac.

Impatient for success, your personal desires come first. You know there's a long road ahead of you, so you're in a hurry to get going.

As the hero in your own adventure, you're the one who wins the day, gets the bravery medal, finds true love and lives happily ever after; at least that's what you expect will happen.

But life often takes us down unexpected roads and for Arians these streets are often paved with large roadblocks and detour signs that seem to have been put there specifically to thwart your every move and make life difficult.

When people first meet you, they know straightaway you're a force to be reckoned with.

Most of these obstacles are there to teach you something, like self-control and that real success comes with persistence, patience and perseverance.

Every time you face a new challenge, you redouble your efforts for you're not going to let anything, or anyone, stand in your way. Failure is simply not an option.

Yet taking action is not always the right thing to do. Why not take the time to pause for a moment and look around and appreciate the scenery along the way? You might also notice there are other people in the world and though you don't care to admit it, some of them are actually wiser than you.

But you just keep rushing into battle, slaying dragons and dashing off to your next conquest. So what happens when the dragon won't give way? What happens when you don't win? When victory can only be attained after years and years of persistent effort, or with some help from other people, how do you cope? And maybe victory will never come, what then? No matter how much courage and energy you have, you are limited by the physical and material world.

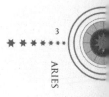

What you need to learn is that to achieve success in any sphere of life there are other approaches worth considering. It's important to plan and think ahead and understand that gentle persuasion is sometimes a better option than full-frontal attack. You also need to choose which battles are worth fighting, for you cannot fight them all.

But how on earth can you do that? How can you remain calm and patient? How can you develop some self-control and restraint and learn to appreciate that there are other ways to approach life's challenges? And how can you possibly decide which battles are worth fighting?

To answer these questions, let's be brave and take an honest look at who you really are.

GIFTS FROM THE PAST

Your sign follows the beautiful waters of Pisces from where all life springs. Pisces is the last sign in the zodiac journey, but you are making a fresh start.

You waste no time in making your desires known and always make the most of any opportunity that comes your way.

Deep inside you lies the cumulative wisdom attained from the long journey through the zodiac, but that's in the past and the past doesn't interest you in the slightest. You're completely focused on the here and now. Direct and to the point, your first instinct is to take the lead.

Pisceans have such a broad universal understanding and make sacrifices for others, but now the tables have turned. Maybe this is why you are so driven; it's like you have been asleep, dreaming all the while of what you would do when given the chance, and now you have woken up.

Once upon a time you believed in magic and miracles, and deep down you still do, but now you only need to believe in yourself.

What you have already learned

- *That you are a spiritual being*
- *To trust your intuition and instinct*
- *That there's a long journey ahead of you*
- *To forgive and forget*
- *That to get anywhere in life, one must fight one's way upstream*
- *To believe in your dreams*
- *To use your imagination*
- *That being totally selfless has some drawbacks*

ELEMENTS OF CHARACTER

Your special place in the zodiac

The first sign

Aries is the first sign of the zodiac. You want to be seen and be heard. The Sun moves into Aries at the spring equinox[1], a time of fresh possibilities and new growth. It's natural for you to be in first place.

You're a pioneer, eager to embark on your mission. You are like a newborn baby who is completely innocent, has enormous potential and energy, yet who also has a lot to learn.

*Aries is arguably the most formidable and dynamic sign
in the whole zodiac.*

You waste no time in making your desires known and always make the most of any opportunity that comes your way.

There's no hidden agenda, no ulterior motive; what everyone sees is what everyone gets. You totally embrace life and live it to the full.

Cardinal fire

Each season commences when the Sun enters one of the four cardinal signs: Aries, Cancer, Libra and Capricorn. These signs of the zodiac are the signs of initiative, leadership and action.

People born with cardinal signs emphasised in their birth charts are born to lead and since Aries is the first sign of the zodiac, you are the most natural leader of all.

*Your first impulse is always to take action, but being
brave and strong doesn't necessarily guarantee you
victory in life, or in love.*

The fire element gives you a liberal dose of spontaneity, creativity and passion, making Aries arguably the most formidable and dynamic sign in the whole zodiac.

Your first impulse is always to take action, but being brave and strong doesn't necessarily guarantee you victory in life, or in love. Sometimes you can also get yourself into trouble, for you often act without thinking. Nevertheless, your motives are true, and you never set out with the deliberate intention of causing harm.

YOUR GODS AND MYTHS

The Romans adopted earlier Greek myths and simply changed the names of the gods and goddesses to Latin. The Greeks too borrowed their myths

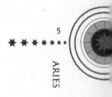

and gods from earlier civilisations, in particular the Babylonians. The themes in myth are universal.

Of all the myths and legends it's the heroic tales which inspire you the most. The hero's journey generally involves a young man who must prove himself worthy and who is given a particular challenge or set of tasks which he must undertake.

> *Of all the myths and legends it's the heroic tales which inspire you the most.*

In many ways everyone's journey through life is a hero's quest, but for you it's special because—more than any other sign—you identify with the archetypal hero.

There are many types of hero; there are anti-heroes, like Robin Hood, who go about doing good deeds, but who act outside the law; and there are unwilling heroes who are forced by fate to take up a quest and in the process find out they are stronger than they thought. But most of all you identify with the hero who must claim his birthright and who must face a number of challenges in order to do so.

However, no matter how brave and strong, the hero doesn't always win. Often a hero has to accept some help along the way, and some heroes must learn what it's like to face defeat.

Mars—God of war

Rome, as the saying goes, was not built in a day, and it certainly would not have been built without its army. Mars is the god of war and the archetype of masculine strength. Mars is energy personified, our drive and ego; without Mars we could never strive for a goal. The month of March is named after him.

As the Roman god of war, Mars was honoured as the father of Romulus and Remus, the founders of Rome.

The Greeks knew him as Ares, who was a more immature and less civilised god than Mars. His aggressive nature made him unpopular, and even his own parents, Zeus and Hera, turned against him.

Ares had a brother, Hephaestus, who was lame and unattractive. Hera banished Hephaestus from heaven because she was ashamed of him. Angry at his mother's treatment, Hephaestus, the blacksmith god, sent his mother a cursed throne so when Hera sat down she was trapped and unable to move.

Rivalry and competition are common themes for Aries natives; in competing with rivals you learn to be strong and independent.

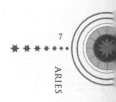

Zeus offered the beautiful Aphrodite in marriage to the god who could free his wife. Aphrodite agreed to this arrangement, thinking that her beloved Ares would prevail but Ares was driven back by showers of flaming metal from his brother's forge.

Dionysus suggested to Hephaestus that he might claim Aphrodite himself if he released his mother willingly, and so the ugly god married the beautiful love goddess.

Aphrodite and Ares were still in love. Ares never married, but he and Aphrodite continued their illicit affair and had several children together.

Rivalry and competition are common themes for Aries natives and although you are not necessarily guaranteed victory in life, or in love, in competing with rivals you learn to be strong and independent.

Jason—The archetypal hero

In order to claim his birthright as the true ruler of Iolcos, Jason was sent by King Pelias on a seemingly impossible quest to claim the Golden Fleece. Jason immediately set about assembling a crew of heroes and built the largest ship ever constructed, the *Argo*.

On the voyage to Colchis, Jason and his crew faced a number of trials and the *Argo* had to pass through treacherous clashing rocks. When they arrived, King Aeetes set Jason yet more tasks before he could claim the Golden Fleece. He had to yoke a team of fire-breathing bulls and use them to plough a field and sow it with dragon's teeth. Then he had to defeat the warriors who sprouted from these teeth-seeds.

Jason managed to perform all the tasks, but still King Aeetes refused to hand over the fleece which would guarantee his birthright.

With the help of the sorceress, Medea, Jason eventually got hold of the fleece. But Jason had even more trials to face because King Pelias had no intention of honouring his promise to give up his throne.

This epic tale tells us there is more to your journey than you might at first assume. Sometimes you need to accept help from others and even when you think you have won victory, that isn't the end of the story.

WHAT YOUR PLANETS REVEAL ABOUT YOU

Though its thin atmosphere is composed mostly of carbon dioxide and its ancient river beds are completely dry, Mars, the red planet, is the most similar planet to Earth.

There's a modern-day myth that the Earth was originally colonised by Martians who came here when their planet was no longer viable. The Martians bred with primitive earthlings thereby creating homosapiens.

True or not, Mars may have once supported life. A meteor, named *Allan Hills 84001*,[2] believed to be from Mars was discovered in Antarctica in 1984. Scientists found the meteor contained remnants of a type of bacteria that travelled here with the meteor some 13 000 years ago.

So it seems that Martians have indeed travelled to the Earth; they were just very small Martians!

The red planet orbits the Sun in a period of 687 days, or a little less than two Earth years, and a day on Mars is around 24½ hours long.

Although Mars is only about half the size of the Earth,
it packs a punch.

Although Mars is only about half the size of the Earth, it packs a punch. Fierce dust storms sweep across its barren landscape and the largest volcano in the entire solar system, Olympus Mons, is found here. It's truly massive; some three times higher than Mt Everest and roughly the size of the state of Victoria or the British Isles.

On 30 October 1938, Orson Welles's *Mercury Theatre on the Air* broadcast an adaptation of the novel by H.G. Wells, *War of the Worlds*. Because the broadcast used a series of documentary-style news reports within its normal music program, audiences across the United States thought the Earth was really being invaded by Martians. It never seems to be Jupiterians or Venusians who want to attack us.

The colour red symbolises war, blood, lust, aggression, energy, power, heat and passion, and so does Mars. In fact it's probably its colour that led to Mars being associated with these qualities from the earliest times.

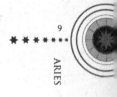

WHAT MAKES YOU TICK?

Aries is like a newborn infant brimming with potential. You have abundant vitality and express yourself with an energy that knows no bounds. You possess physical strength and emotional intensity in equal measure and you can't wait to experience all that life has to offer.

The here and now is where the action is and that's
where you want to be.

Like a superhero, you have a deep-seated feeling of omnipotence which comes from the vast and universal realm of Pisces.

Although in many ways Pisces is your polar opposite because it's at the end of the zodiac while you are at the start, you can call on its wisdom to make your dreams come true.

> *You possess physical strength and emotional intensity in equal measure and you can't wait to experience all that life has to offer.*

When you were a kid you were probably into every kind of adventure; climbing trees, tearing around on your bike and generally behaving like Dennis the Menace. Aries children insist on getting their own way and are often hyperactive. These are the children you see throwing balls at the park or tantrums in the supermarket. Aries girls are often tomboys. Aries children are often unwilling to go to bed at bedtime and will protest loudly. This is because they're worried they'll miss out on all the action. Insomnia can be a problem for Aries adults too.

Your first instinct is to jump right in and tackle problems head on for you know that actions speak louder than words. The typical Arian has a tendency to be impulsive and to jump to conclusions. Your enthusiasm can make you overreact.

> *Aries children insist on getting their own way and are often hyperactive.*

Everything you undertake you do wholeheartedly. You're ultra-confident and will stop at nothing, but at the same time you're generous to a fault. You're not the slightest bit ruthless or vindictive, but you can be pushy.

In others' eyes your generosity and honesty go a long way to make up for your occasional chest-beating. You speak your mind and can be argumentative at times, but you never carry a grudge. You always forgive and forget.

Daffy Duck made his screen debut on 17 April 1937, which makes him an Aries; hot-tempered, fearless and argumentative, he desires to win at all costs.

One of Daffy's most famous roles was in *Duck Dodgers in the 24½th Century*. Daffy and his sidekick Porky, an eager young space cadet, travel to Planet X looking for the last known source of the shaving-cream atom, Illudium Phosdex. As soon as Daffy claims Planet X in the name of the Earth, Marvin the Martian arrives and claims it for Mars. Daffy and Marvin fight it out and eventually succeed in blowing Planet X to bits. Never one to admit defeat, Daffy claims what is left of Planet X anyway.

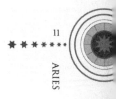

You know that actions speak louder than words.

When under threat in the heat of battle, adrenaline kicks in to provide more energy. Blood pumps harder, making you capable of superhuman strength. Mars represents the 'fight or flight' reaction.

Most of the time you choose to fight rather than flee. Being headstrong can make you prone to angry outbursts now and then, but mostly these are short-lived.

However, when you run into obstacles you can feel stressed and tense, especially if your energy has no outlet. The result can be headaches, fevers, heartburn, insomnia, infections, high blood pressure, or inflammatory conditions.

Aries people make great sales people. You're great at selling yourself and your ideas too.

Aries people tend to carry too much heat in their bodies and quite a number have a ruddy complexion or red hair. Alcohol and stimulants can create havoc with your system and should be kept to a minimum, or avoided completely.

Chances are you excel at sport or activities requiring physical bravery, and you may have your fair share of accidents too, especially when young. You tend to overestimate your strength and underestimate who or what you are up against. Broken bones and head injuries can result, because in your enthusiasm you do not properly evaluate the likely risk.

While it's important for you to have an outlet for your abundant energy, at the same time you need to recognise that you are not really Superman or Wonder Woman. As you get older it may be difficult for you to accept that you are not as strong and youthful as you once were.

You dislike taking direction from others because you are fiercely independent and like to be in charge. When learning something new, you don't like being told what to do—you learn by doing it yourself. On the whole you are more interested in the action itself, rather than the end result.

Many highly creative people are born with Aries strong in their birth charts. When it comes to work, you are suited to any kind of creative enterprise. Since you are a natural leader, it makes sense for you to work for yourself.

You know you are destined for great things. Whatever you undertake you do with courage and the conviction that you will triumph.

Aries people make great sales people. You're great at selling yourself and your ideas too. Apart from self-employment and creative occupations, Aries people are also drawn to work that involves daring and adventure, such as the police force or the military, but here again you can get into trouble because following rules and taking orders are not your strong suits.

An Aries client of mine works in a highly paid, quite dangerous job, but only takes on short-term contracts. He prefers this to regular employment because then he has enough time and energy to fight for some important causes that are close to his heart.

You are motivated by challenges and the desire to win, rather than by money. In fact, having to deal with money and the material world can be a problem for you. Like Robin Hood (Daffy Duck played this role too), you love the idea of robbing from the rich and giving to the poor. As far as you are concerned, money is there to be spent. You're not interested in saving your pennies for a rainy day. The here and now is where the action is and that's where you want to be.

One day you might decide to work for yourself, if only it wasn't necessary to put down a business plan on paper, for you find this tedious in the extreme. You just want to get on with the creative part.

But if you need to raise capital for your particular enterprise, you're going to have to get a handle on the financial aspects of the business. A partnership or joint venture might be an option, but what you really want is a silent partner, someone who puts up the capital, pays the bills and leaves the rest to you.

You know you are destined for great things. Aries people are among the most successful people in the world. Whatever you undertake in life you do with courage and the conviction that you will triumph, and you usually do.

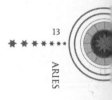

THE REALLY IMPORTANT THINGS IN YOUR LIFE

Romantic adventure

Sexually, you're a dynamo—with Mars as your ruling planet how could it be otherwise? Both Aries men and women are equally passionate.

The glyph for Aries ♈ symbolises the ram's horns, a potent symbol of masculinity, fertility and power.

Women with Aries or Mars strongly positioned at birth seek equality with men in every aspect.

Ninety-nine per cent of the time you are the one who does the pursuing. Male or female, you go after who you most desire, and will not take no for an answer. You will send roses, give lavish gifts and always go out of your way to help those you love—nothing is too much to ask.

Like Sagittarians, at times you can behave like a veritable Don Juan, but once you give your heart to someone, you give it totally.

You wear your heart on your sleeve and seek true love. You are looking for the one special person who will win your heart.

Some people are intimidated by your full-on approach but you win them over with your charm, honesty and winning smile. It might seem like a contradiction for such a strong and forceful sign, but Aries is one of the most romantic signs in the whole zodiac.

You wear your heart on your sleeve and seek true love. You are looking for the one special person who will win your heart.

Women with Aries or Mars strongly positioned at birth seek equality with men in every aspect. They are the original feminists of the zodiac, but find it challenging to express their ambitions in a world that is still largely dominated by men, some of whom feel threatened by independent, assertive women. But Aries men generally don't fall into this category. They have a stronger ego than that and respect strength in others, plus they are usually seeking a relationship based on equality. Male or female, you prefer people who stand up to you.

Venus and Mars are the lovers of the zodiac, and because Venus rules Taurus, which is the sign after yours, and also Libra, your opposite sign, there is a powerful magnetism which pulls you towards love and beauty wherever it might be found. Love softens your rough edges and soothes your soul, plus helps you learn more about relationships and people. Romance is the way to enduring love.

It's all part of the great adventure that is your life. If you are not chasing after your true love, then you are racing fast cars, pitting yourself against all-comers, or, like Harry Houdini, planning your next death-defying act.

People look to you for leadership, inspiration and courage.

You expect to win the day, and win the love of your life, for you know it's the bravest and truest, the most honourable knight who wins the hand of the fair maiden and the medal for valour.

You set an example by showing others how to have the courage of their convictions. No matter how big the challenge, you take it on with gusto.

Just as they look to Superman, Robin Hood and countless other heroes, people look to you for leadership, inspiration and courage.

SHARING YOUR KNOWLEDGE

How you get along with others

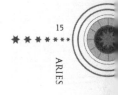

People you can teach:	Water signs—Cancer, Scorpio, Pisces
Compatible similar signs:	Fire signs—Aries, Leo, Sagittarius
Compatible complementary signs:	Air signs—Gemini, Libra, Aquarius
People you can learn from:	Earth signs—Taurus, Virgo, Capricorn

Relating to water signs (Cancer, Scorpio, Pisces)

You have an intrinsic understanding of the water signs—Pisces, Cancer and Scorpio—and go out of your way to help these people.

Because you have the drive and enthusiasm they lack, you are generous towards them. You are always at the ready to give them a confidence boost and to motivate them.

However, water signs don't like being pushed. On the whole they feel you are too aggressive and are putting them under pressure. They recoil and retreat, and don't feel at all comfortable when on the receiving end of your encouragement, which they interpret as hostility and aggression, making them resistant to your valiant attempts to get them moving.

Water/Fire relationships tend to be very emotionally charged and volatile because water can extinguish fire, while fire can make water boil and evaporate.

Relating to fire signs (Aries, Leo, Sagittarius)

Many of your good friends are probably fire signs. They are your astrological brothers and sisters. You share similar values and interests. Sometimes relationships between fire signs can become overheated, even potentially destructive, for fire signs can become very competitive with one another.

Still, you have a great deal in common. You will probably develop great friendships with Leos, Sagittarians and other Arians, but it is important to realise that things can quickly get out of hand when you spend too much time together.

Relating to air signs (Gemini, Libra, Aquarius)

Potentially, relationships with the air signs are the happiest relationships you will ever have. Air signs bring you opportunities and contacts that can help you to achieve success. Plus they are rational thinkers and enjoy taking care of the details that you often have trouble managing.

You are not alone in being curious about your opposite sign. It's true that opposites attract, so you are probably fascinated by Librans.

Librans can be truly supportive and help you get your projects off the ground, but they can drive you crazy because they take so long to make a decision. They value relationships more than individual initiatives, while you value independence more than relationships and never stop to consult other people.

Librans are always seeking consensus and diplomatic compromises which frustrates you to the point where you just explode. You're passionate and emotional, while they are cool, intellectual and rational. Relationships between opposite signs often bring out the best and worst in people.

Relating to earth signs (Taurus, Virgo, Capricorn)

Earth signs are the people who are always putting up roadblocks in front of you, but they are here to teach you to be more practical and help you navigate through the clashing rocks of the material world. They know that slower, sustained effort over time can make a real difference. You need to learn that slow and steady often wins the race. When you experience conflicts with the earth signs, you are learning how to deal with limitations and responsibilities.

WHAT YOU NEED TO LEARN

Patience

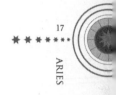

Although you have a battalion of enthusiasm and courage, you have to admit that you have a short attention span and an even shorter fuse. If immediate gratification is not forthcoming, like any normal 2-year-old you tend to spit the dummy; but when you do that, you can actually end up defeating yourself.

When you have to wait your turn you become frustrated and have nowhere to put all your energy. It's like a recurring dream where you run and run as hard as you can, but get nowhere fast.

What you need to learn is to have patience. You need to remain calm and endure your impatience without allowing your passions to spur you to action. What! See, there you go, getting all hot under the collar. But when the traffic lights turn red, it's usually for a very good reason. Sometimes red means stop.

When you have to wait your turn, like any normal 2-year-old you have a tendency to spit the dummy.

You'd rather push forward with all your drive and initiative, put yourself to the test and compete. In short, you want to do things *your* way. But as you get older you'll begin to see that you don't have all the answers. You will be forced to admit it, because by then you will have suffered a number of defeats. And to your great annoyance it's the earth signs who are generally the ones who beat you. Yes, those stodgy Taureans, those nitpicking Virgos and those rule-obsessed Capricorns.

The earth signs of this world are great at managing the reality of time and space. They're highly resourceful and have the capacity for endurance that you don't.

There really is no point throwing a tantrum when you don't immediately get what you want. No matter how brave and courageous you are, or how much energy you exert, and regardless of how much enthusiasm and initiative you show, sometimes you will be forced to withdraw.

All the chest-beating in the world isn't going to help
you when you are standing before a brick wall.

All the chest-beating in the world isn't going to help you when you are standing before a brick wall. However many times you hit your head against it, all you succeed in doing is giving yourself a head injury.

Eventually, you'll start to get the idea that maybe another approach is required.

TAKING THE NEXT STEP

It's hard for you to accept, but it's the earth signs of the world who often succeed where you fail. You? Fail? Never! I know it's difficult to admit, but the fact remains that sometimes you do. Earth signs have the self-discipline, the tenacity and the patience for the long haul. They're good organisers, hard workers and are responsible and orderly. In short, they have the tools you need.

Earth signs manage the material world with ease. They know we all have to pay our dues and that to achieve what we want in life takes both effort and time. You don't mind putting in the effort, but it's the time thing that you have trouble accepting.

It might slowly dawn on you that you
cannot fight every battle; you must choose which
ones to take up.

The good news is that the earth signs want to teach you what you need to know. They really admire your daring, energy and creativity, and they also understand where you are coming from.

Think of them as very old and very wise fire sign people, who no longer have the physical energy they once possessed but have developed the wisdom that comes with maturity. When you reach old age, you might be like them.

However, you tend to think earth signs are slow and dull and couldn't possibly have any knowledge or advice that might help you.

As you find yourself facing an opponent or situation you cannot overcome, it might slowly dawn on you that you cannot fight every battle; you must choose which ones to take up. But in order to do this, you must first develop a set of priorities and values. This will help you decide which battles are worth fighting.

All earth signs appreciate your dynamic creativity
and fearlessness.

Taurus is the sign that follows yours so these people know about values. Although they cause you the most frustration of all the signs, they can teach you to prioritise and how to develop some stamina and endurance. Not that you see it that way. To you, Taureans are either lazy, incredibly slow, or stick-in-the-muds.

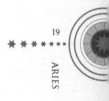

But just like you want to help the water signs to be more confident and outgoing, the earth signs want you to develop practical skills, self-discipline, patience and restraint.

On your hero's quest, try to realise that obstacles are not there just to annoy you, but to teach you something. You are never going to turn into a Taurus, but just like Daffy Duck, you can evolve over time.

TIPS FOR ARIES

♈ Recognise that developing some patience can help you win.
♈ Take up a hobby that involves manual hands-on work.
♈ Every so often, let others go first.
♈ Be gracious in defeat.
♈ When you feel frustrated, realise you are actually angry with yourself.
♈ Open a savings account and make regular deposits.
♈ Consider the advice of the earth signs you meet.

YOUR GIFT TO THE WORLD

How you can make a real difference

Your special gift to the world is your bravery and leadership. Where others fear to stand up, you don't hesitate for a second. You inspire others with your daring. If every soul on planet Earth were an Aries, things would get done. There'd be no procrastination, no time-wasting and no red tape.

You are a source of inspiration to those who have neither the strength nor the initiative to stand up for themselves. Though you are just setting out and have a long journey ahead, your boundless enthusiasm and courage set you apart, and show that every single one of us is a hero in our own way and that we can each make a big difference.

FAMOUS PERSONALITIES WITH THE SUN IN ARIES INCLUDE:

Alec Baldwin
Marlon Brando
Joseph Campbell
Jackie Chan
Charlie Chaplin
Russell Crowe
Francis Ford Coppola
Daffy Duck
Bette Davis
Jane Goodall
Al Gore
Harry Houdini

Thomas Jefferson
Heath Ledger
Jayne Mansfield
Marcel Marceau
Ewan McGregor
Steve McQueen
Spike Milligan
Gloria Steinem
Quentin Tarantino
Vincent Van Gogh
Reese Witherspoon
Angus Young

TAURUS

21 APRIL–21 MAY

'Common sense is that which judges the things
given to it by other senses.'

TAURUS, LEONARDO DA VINCI

YOUR LIFE MISSION

To have worthwhile values upon which you can depend. To preserve these standards and build something that provides security.

The second step in the zodiac journey involves making practical use of the energy, drive and passion of Aries, by building something lasting and permanent. This is where you come in.

Though to others you can seem at times to be overly focused on money and possessions, it's no mean feat to master the material world. Let's be honest, nobody aspires to poverty. Without food and shelter we cannot thrive, let alone make use of our talents, and you have many talents that you want to utilise.

Every Taurus wants to build something solid in life; something that will endure and provide lasting security. Though you want material success, it's not really money and possessions which motivate you. Being financially secure might be what you wish for, but it's your underlying values which really sustain you, and they don't come with a price tag.

Your values are the rudder that steers your decision-making in all spheres of life.

Depending on a number of factors in your birth chart, for instance the location of your ruling planet, Venus, every Taurus has a very personal and individual style and a particular method of evaluation.

Without food and shelter we cannot thrive, let alone make use of our talents, and you have many talents that you want to utilise.

Whatever your value system, you stay loyal to your principles, for then you have a firm foundation which provides the certainty and security that is so important to you. However, this means you tend to evaluate everything according to these same particular standards, to the point where you fail to take into account the tremendous diversity of ideas that exist in the world.

Change is not something you handle particularly well. You find it especially annoying when people keep moving the goalposts. Why change what works? You'd prefer it if everyone were cut from the same cloth and things just stayed as they are.

As new ideas and information become available, you find it hard to adapt. You're not interested in changing or adapting, because as far as you're concerned, your standards are the best and most worthwhile so you prefer to stick with the tried and true.

So when things change, as they always do, you can become intransigent. You can even become judgemental, labelling anything unfamiliar as completely worthless.

So how can you build something that really endures? When your values become outmoded by new styles, new trends and fresh information, how do you cope with these changes? And is it possible to maintain your position while learning to be more adaptable?

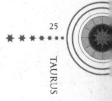

GIFTS FROM THE PAST

If you are born with the Sun in Taurus, it means you have inherited lots of Aries energy. You have strength and courage. Now you can call on these Aries qualities as you begin your journey to master the material world.

What you have already learned

- *That you have courage*
- *To go after what you desire most*
- *What it's like to be first*
- *To be assertive*
- *That you are strong*

- ✸ *To have confidence in your own abilities*
- ✸ *To be self-reliant and independent*
- ✸ *That acting on impulse is not always desirable*

ELEMENTS OF CHARACTER

Your special place in the zodiac

The second sign

Just as the first sign of the zodiac is like the newborn infant, innocent and full of energy, the second sign is where that child becomes aware of its surroundings and finds a way to have its needs met.

Your sign is the most sensual sign of all.

Taurus is about the relationship between you and the outside world. In Taurus the focus is very much on the physical senses—taste, touch, smell, sight and hearing. For it's through the senses that we evaluate the outside world and make sense of it.

Consequently, you appreciate everything that stimulates the senses; in fact your sign is the most sensual sign of all.

Fixed earth

The Sun is in Taurus at the height of spring, when the land is ripe, fertile and beautiful.

Like those born under the other earth signs, Virgo and Capricorn, you appreciate the beauty of nature. All earth signs are practical, reliable and realistic, but as Taurus is also a fixed sign, this makes you incredibly resilient too. Therefore, Taurus is the most fixed of the fixed signs because its element is earth.

Fixity and earth combine to make you the most persistent and indeed stubborn sign of the zodiac. Nothing and no one can shift you an inch unless you want to be moved, and that's not often. You stand your ground and go at your own pace.

As the first earth sign, it's up to you to identify, evaluate and establish reliable standards. These benchmarks will evolve in the next earth sign, Virgo, where they will be honed and perfected, and in Capricorn, where they will be expanded upon and given wider application, becoming the rules that govern behaviour throughout society as a whole—so you know the importance of having a firm foundation upon which to build.

YOUR GODS AND MYTHS

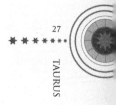

There is a deep mystery at the heart of Taurus; your sign is a feminine sign, ruled by the beautiful love goddess Venus, but your motif is that of the bull, also a symbol of fertility, but arguably the most masculine symbol in the entire zodiac. Your sign has two distinct faces, a combination of masculine strength and feminine beauty.

While every person and every zodiac sign is a mix of good and bad, somehow positive and negative seem to be more polarised in Taurus than in any other sign. This probably has something to do with the strongly fixed nature of your sign, which makes you prone to stick with the devil you know.

Venus—Goddess of love and beauty

The goddess of love and beauty, Venus/Aphrodite, was born in the foaming sea where Saturn/Cronus[1] had thrown the castrated sex organs of his father Uranus. As her birth would suggest, the goddess of love was both beautiful and sexual. The word 'aphrodisiac' comes from Aphrodite.

Your sign has two distinct faces, a combination of
masculine strength and feminine beauty.

In the famous story of the Judgement of Paris, all the gods and goddesses except Eris, the goddess of discord, were invited to the wedding of Peleus and Thetis. Angry at her exclusion, Eris tossed a golden apple inscribed 'to the fairest' to the wedding party. Hera, Athena and Aphrodite all claimed the apple.

In order to settle the dispute, Zeus selected the Trojan prince, Paris, to decide the matter. Each goddess offered Paris a bribe. Hera and Athena offered him victory and power, but Aphrodite offered him the most beautiful mortal woman, Helen of Troy, so Paris declared Aphrodite to be the fairest.

However, this declaration had drastic consequences for it led to the Trojan War, in which all the gods and goddesses took sides.

Aphrodite was on the side of the Trojans and was even wounded in the ensuing battle. Although Aphrodite was declared the fairest, ultimately she ended up on the losing side, which goes to show that even if you are the most talented or worthy, making judgements about who is the best can result in conflict. Even if you win the battle, you might still lose the war.

The white bull

The bull is a potent symbol of fertility and power. One myth tells how Minos asked the gods for a sign that they favoured his claim to the kingdom of Crete. Poseidon agreed to send him a white bull to show his support. The condition was that Minos should sacrifice the bull to honour Poseidon for his favour, but after he became king, Minos decided to keep the magnificent beast for himself and sacrificed another bull of inferior quality.

In retaliation, Poseidon caused the king's wife to lust after the bull. She mated with it and bore a hideous creature called the Minotaur, which had a human body and the head of a bull. It was hidden away in a labyrinth, where it feasted on human flesh.

There is an important lesson in this story, especially for Taureans, for when greed takes hold, dark forces are often unleashed.

WHAT YOUR PLANETS REVEAL ABOUT YOU

After the Sun and the Moon, Venus is the brightest object in the sky. It's almost a perfect sphere and has the most circular orbit of all the planets, hence its association with beauty.

A Venus year is 225 days long, compared to our year of 365 days which is shown in the ratio of 5:8, or 1.618: the Golden Ratio.[2]

The Golden Ratio is considered aesthetically pleasing and was used extensively in Classical and Renaissance art and architecture.

One of the greatest artists of all time, Leonardo da Vinci, who was born with both the Sun and Venus in Taurus, used the Golden Ratio in much of his work.

The Mayans also recognised the special relationship between Venus and the Earth and based their calendar on the cycle of Venus.

Venus spends around 260 days as the morning star and the same amount of time as the evening star. One of the reasons Venus is associated with fertility is because 260 days is very close to the length of a human gestation period.

Venus is beautiful; a dazzling diamond in the night sky,
but up close it's a hideous place.

The so-called 'Earth's twin', Venus is the closest planet to the Earth, and about the same size, but that is where any similarity ends.

Oddly, a day on Venus is actually longer than its year. It rotates backwards on its axis incredibly slowly, which means if you were standing on Venus the Sun would rise in the west and stay up in the sky for several months[3] before setting in the east. But you wouldn't actually see the Sun, because Venus is covered by thick clouds which reflect the Sun's light back into space, but trap its heat.

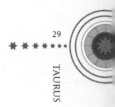

✹ ✹ ✹ ✹ ✹ ✹ ✹

TAURUS

Venus is beautiful; a dazzling diamond in the night sky, but up close it's a hideous place with a toxic atmosphere of carbon dioxide and sulphuric acid. The atmospheric pressure is 90 times stronger than on Earth, and though Mercury is closer to the Sun, Venus is the hottest place in the solar system, hot enough to melt lead, even at night.

Again we can see the two faces of Venus, one pure and beautiful, the other dark and nasty.

Venus traces a five pointed star, a pentagram, as it moves through the zodiac over an eight year period. In the tarot deck, pentagrams also represent material wealth and the earth element, both key aspects of Taurus.

Venus is never more than 48 degrees away from the Sun, which means it's always in the same sign as the Sun, or in one of the two signs before or after the Sun. For example, if your Sun sign is Taurus, then Venus can only be located in one of five signs: Pisces, Aries, Taurus, Gemini or Cancer.

The position of Venus in your natal chart will modify the type of Taurus you are. For example, the beautiful Michele Pfeiffer has Venus in Pisces, adding a gentle watery feel to her feminine expression. Katharine Hepburn was a good example of a Taurus with Venus in Aries; independent, outspoken and forthright. Look to your Venus sign for deeper insight into your values, relationships and personal style.

WHAT MAKES YOU TICK?

The fixity of your sign makes you incredibly stubborn. It's a behaviour Taurus children learn as they try to exert influence over their world. Mostly, these kids are orderly and well-behaved and always take good care of their possessions. However, they're known to throw the occasional temper tantrum, or hold their breath in order to get their own way, especially when they want a food treat and Mum won't buy it for them. If you have Taurus children it's a good idea to feed them before you take them supermarket shopping.

> *Lots of hugs and affection strengthens the Taurus self-esteem, resulting in a loving and charismatic individual.*

The first day of school is another time when the Taurus child might stamp their foot and point-blank refuse to go, but once they know there will be painting and other creative activities, they're usually willing to give it a try.

These youngsters sometimes have trouble adjusting to new routines. Learning new things means having to adapt and this can make the young Taurean feel insecure, at least initially, but life soon settles down into a regular pattern and the Taurus child is all smiles again and really starts to thrive.

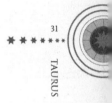

In June 2004, we witnessed a rare transit of Venus, when Venus crossed directly in front of the Sun. Transits of Venus are rare because the Earth and Venus move in different planes of orbit. Before 2004, the previous transit of Venus was in 1882. Transits of Venus occur in pairs, eight years apart, so we will witness another one in June 2012.

This will happen in Gemini, bringing fresh opportunities for personal growth in the years to come.

All earth signs, children and adults alike, need routine and order, and Taurus most of all. Having a stable home life is particularly important.

Lots of hugs and displays of affection strengthen the Taurus self-esteem too, resulting in a self-sufficient, loving and charismatic individual.

Many Taureans are physically beautiful, with strong, yet graceful bodies like dancers Fred Astaire and Margot Fonteyn, who were known for their discipline and stamina. Gifted artists often have Taurus emphasised in their birth charts.

> *You have the necessary endurance and stamina to reach success in any field.*

Singers like Bing Crosby and Ella Fitzgerald are good examples of the resonant Taurus voice, which is not surprising because the neck and throat are the parts of the body associated with your sign.

Many great chefs are born under your sign too. When preparing a sumptuous banquet for friends or family, you go to great lengths to make sure everything is just right, and even more so when you are planning a romantic dinner for two.

Soft candlelight and beautiful music, the best in food and wine, a long back and neck massage using essential oils to stimulate the senses, followed by passionate love-making is your idea of heaven. It's a toss-up which room of the house is your favourite, the kitchen or the bedroom.

Eating, making love and sleeping are all favourite Taurean pastimes, and not necessarily in that order. Breakfast in bed and sex in the kitchen are often on the menu.

All Taureans love food and many have a sweet tooth which can make the average Taurean prone to weight gain.

> *Eating, making love and sleeping are favourite Taurean pastimes, and not necessarily in that order. Breakfast in bed and sex in the kitchen are often on the menu.*

My adorable Taurus dog never leaves a scrap of food and when he wants more, which is all the time, he stands in the kitchen and literally stamps his foot. His beautiful black velvet ears flop forward and he looks at me with his big brown puppy dog eyes; all the while pointing his nose firmly in the direction of the dog treats. As much as he loves me, without a doubt he loves food more.

Like all Taureans, anything associated with Gemini can be an issue, and the postman definitely falls into this category. You too are apt to bark and growl when someone comes along with new information, for you are trying to protect your turf.

But you need to know that the old adage 'You can't teach an old dog new tricks' isn't true. Whoever said that animals weren't intelligent wasn't very smart. Even the most stubborn Taurus bull can learn to adapt over time.

The unconditional love that dogs give to humans is the kind of loyalty you are famous for. No other sign of the zodiac is as loyal or loving.

But loyalty is so important to you that when people disagree with you, you can take it as a personal affront. When loved ones don't go along with you, you can feel betrayed and act as if they're disloyal, when in reality they're only being true to their own values, just as you are.

The unconditional love that dogs give to people is just like the kind of loyalty you are famous for.

As your Libran friends will tell you, there are two sides to everything, but you don't see it that way. As far as you're concerned, you have already made up your mind, and once you do, you stick to your guns, no matter what.

This gives your sign the reputation for being rather pig-headed, but it also means you have the necessary endurance, persistence and stamina to reach success in any field. You never give up.

Your tremendous determination and resilience makes you the most persistent sign of the zodiac. You're patient, practical and resourceful, and you can make a little go a very long way.

Though you are conservative and usually agree with the majority view, even when you are in the minority you have no hesitation in standing up for yourself and your opinions, or your loved ones, never flinching for a second in your convictions.

However it's also worth noting that Lucrezia Borgia,[4] Adolf Hitler and Saddam Hussein were all Taureans, which goes to show what can happen when the dark side of Taurus takes hold.

On the other side of the Taurus fence are the truly beautiful people of the world; people like the graceful Audrey Hepburn and the charming George Clooney; those who know that beauty is not skin deep and that one's true worth comes from deep within the soul.

THE REALLY IMPORTANT THINGS IN YOUR LIFE

Material security

I know two Taurean sisters who were born a year apart and who have never seen eye to eye on anything. Apparently, the problem started when they were children, they just never got on.

The younger sister spares no expense and always buys the most expensive products, assured her money is well spent. She is certain that good labels mean superior quality. The elder sister, although incredibly generous towards others, hardly ever spends any money on herself, and when she does, always worries about how expensive everything seems to be.

However you choose to spend your hard-earned money, you have the uncanny knack of buying items that increase in value.

They are always reminding me of how very different they are from one another. The younger one asserts that clearly this means that astrology has no merit whatsoever, while the other is convinced that she is the true Taurus and that there must have been a mix-up with her sister's birth certificate. Each is convinced without a doubt that they are right and the other is wrong.

However you choose to spend your hard-earned money, you have the uncanny knack of buying items that increase in value. Taureans are canny investors and good at saving too. Investing in bricks and mortar is probably more appealing to you than the share market, but it's no accident that a growing share market is called a 'bull market'.

On the whole the average Taurus is more interested in security and comfort than in accumulating money for its own sake.

It's often the case that Taureans experience great poverty and/or great wealth. While nobody wants to be uncomfortable, hungry or poor, least of all you, you also know that money can't buy love, and that's more important.

Banker, real estate agent, accountant, fashion designer, chef, masseur, beauty therapist, farmer, property developer, builder or tradesperson are just some of the many occupations that might appeal. You have so many skills and talents that when it comes to earning a living you have lots of options.

You are dedicated to your work, but expect to be compensated accordingly. You have no qualms in asking for a pay rise, or for fringe benefits, and you usually manage to get what you want, for you know your true worth.

The average Taurus prefers to stay in the one job for a considerable time; once upon a time everyone did. At the end of 40 years' service, you got your gold watch and sat back to enjoy retirement. These days, people move around a lot more, even changing careers, but this is not usually the case with Taureans.

It's no accident that a growing share market is called a 'bull market'.

Although you have many talents, you prefer the security of a regular pay cheque so you can build a large nest egg. When retirement does come, you can truly enjoy the fruits of your labours.

The material world often tests us, but you are determined to pass these tests. Whether rich or poor, it's the mission of every Taurus to come to terms with money, so that money is not the root of all evil, nor a limitation that prevents you from thriving, but is used to build something lasting and beautiful which has more intrinsic value than the dollars that went into it.

By mastering the material world you learn what is truly of value.

While the negative side of your sign can be overly materialistic, you know deep down that not everything comes with a price tag. By mastering the material world you learn what is truly of value and discover the most valuable thing of all—unconditional love.

SHARING YOUR KNOWLEDGE

How you get along with others

People you can teach:	Fire signs—Aries, Leo, Sagittarius
Compatible similar signs:	Earth signs—Taurus, Virgo, Capricorn
Compatible complementary signs:	Water signs—Cancer, Scorpio, Pisces
People you can learn from:	Air signs—Gemini, Libra, Aquarius

Relating to fire signs (Aries, Leo, Sagittarius)

Because Aries is the sign before Taurus you have a good understanding of the fire signs. On the whole you are sympathetic towards them and want to teach them the skills they lack.

Since you are practical and manage the material world with relative ease, you can teach the fire signs to be more thorough, orderly, persistent and patient. Your down-to-earth, commonsense approach makes you the right person to show them how to handle money and finances and it's pretty obvious they need all the help they can get. You instinctively know how to turn their creative ideas into practical outcomes. If only they would listen!

> *You instinctively know how to turn creative ideas into practical outcomes.*

Relating to fire signs can be difficult. While you want them to grow and evolve, there are some stark differences between you, which often results in conflict. Nevertheless, you are generous towards them and give in to them more frequently than you do with others.

Basically, you want them to be more like you. Unfortunately, that's unlikely to happen, at least in the short-term, but you never give up. Fire/Earth relationships are often challenging, but despite your many differences you still find fire signs highly desirable.

Relating to earth signs (Taurus, Virgo, Capricorn)

All earth signs share similar values. You're reliable, responsible, diligent and practical. Because of these similarities, your relationships with other earth signs are generally stable and long lived. Earth signs don't like change that much, though Virgos and Capricorns are probably a tad more open to change than you, but all of you like to have clear parameters in which to operate.

Virgo is a mutable sign and has Mercury as a ruling planet. This makes them skilled communicators who can teach you to be more adaptable, without the conflict that you normally encounter with air signs. Although Virgos can find your stubbornness a little difficult to deal with at times, they will gently encourage you to try new things.

While relationships between earth signs are mutually beneficial, because earth signs like routine, you can end up falling into a rut when you spend a lot of time together. Nevertheless, you always manage to find common ground.

Relating to water signs (Cancer, Scorpio, Pisces)

Potentially, relationships with the water signs are the most beautiful experiences you will ever encounter. Water and earth are naturally compatible elements, for water nurtures earth and earth gives structure and form to water. Cancerians and Pisceans are particularly compatible with Taureans, while Scorpio is your opposite sign, and we can all learn something from our opposing sign.

While opposites do attract, and we can all learn something from our opposite sign, the problems are magnified too.

Scorpios can be incredible sexy and charismatic, but because you are both fixed signs, neither of you finds compromise easy. Scorpios are deep and they have their secrets, so trust, possessiveness and jealousy can be issues and arguments over money can erupt. Consequently, Taurus/Scorpio relationships can be destructive in the long run.

Relating to air signs (Gemini, Libra, Aquarius)

Air signs drive you crazy because they are always on the move and making changes. They frustrate you no end because they are always changing their tune for no particular logical reason. In direct proportion, the more inflexible and stubborn you are, the more changeable and erratic are the people and situations you encounter. But air signs can teach you a thing or two if you are willing to learn.

WHAT YOU NEED TO LEARN

To keep an open mind

Though you have patience, reliability, loyalty and numerous other attributes, when it comes to adapting to new situations, you struggle.

The sign that follows yours, Gemini, is the sign of communication and travel, so moving around from place to place can really unsettle you. Maybe you actually get car sick. Taureans can be very nervous passengers. Fear of flying is also a common Taurus problem. But these issues can be helped when you understand more about Gemini and the air element.

Being true to your values is of paramount importance, and your self-esteem is based on your adherence to these principles.

> *Communication can help resolve disputes, and to really communicate, you need to listen, not just give your own opinions.*

You tend to make judgement calls which fail to take into account that each and every person is on their own special journey. Each person is different and capable of change, and that includes you.

Whatever your particular values, the important thing as far as you are concerned is to stick with them. Whether you evaluate things according to their physical beauty, social merit, taste, or some kind of sixth sense, you are always giving things a rating. Where does this new experience, person, object, or piece of information fit into your rating system?

And if it doesn't fit into your notion of what is valuable, you often dismiss it as unworthy or unimportant.

It never occurs to you that standards and values change with new experiences, learning and knowledge. The more information we have, the more conscious we become, but you don't see it that way. It's hard for you to accept there are values other than your own. You are so certain that yours are the best that you can close your mind to new information, and when that happens, you run the risk of becoming so intransigent that you let the dark side of Taurus take over.

Communication can help resolve disputes, and to really communicate, you need to listen, not just give your own opinions. Communication helps you move beyond your fixity and see there are other viewpoints. In the process you learn to adapt and become more flexible, which makes you stronger.

TAURUS

You know that it takes a lot of time and effort for a seed to grow into a tree. You always plant your seeds in fertile soil, provide them with love and care, so your trees thrive and grow strong, but even the biggest trees still bend in the wind.

You always plant your seeds in fertile soil, provide them with love and care, so your tree thrives and grows up strong with a healthy root system.

Air signs are like the wind, and they are trying to teach you to bend. As you start to move, they will help you distribute your new seeds, scattering them far and wide, leading to new growth.

Yes, the wind can be annoying—sometimes it blows hot and other times cold, sometimes it's still and other times it's a howling gale—but you can't stop it from blowing.

TAKING THE NEXT STEP

Being the practical person you are, you have to face the fact that change happens. Things just don't stay the same, no matter how much you want them to.

Just like you want to help the fire signs to develop their talents and build something lasting, the air signs want to teach you to adapt.

But all this to-ing and fro-ing makes you feel insecure because different viewpoints and values, and the people who have them, seem to undermine the established framework and standards upon which your life is constructed.

Like Venus itself, which rotates backwards on its axis very slowly, it can be hard for you to move forward. What you need to know is that you can learn to deal with change and different points of view by allowing the air signs to educate you. Just like you want to help the fire signs to develop their talents and build something lasting, the air signs want to teach you to adapt.

In fact, the more inflexible you are, the more changeable and erratic are the people and situations you invariably encounter. This is a law of nature, and since you appreciate nature, you can also learn to keep an open mind.

A little flexibility on your part goes a long way.

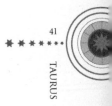

Librans have Venus as a ruling planet just like you, but as an air sign they can teach you a great deal. Relationships, beauty and art are just as important to Librans as they are to you, but they can teach you how to communicate, cooperate and share.

Relationships with Aquarians are not easy, mostly because you are both fixed signs, so Aquarians have their way of doing things, and you have yours. They will try to get you to change, but this only makes you dig in your heels.

You are quite comfortable doing things your own way, but the more you interact with air signs, the more you will come to see there are alternatives and options available to you. You don't have to give up your values, possessions or your creature comforts, nor compromise if you don't want to, but a little flexibility on your part goes a long way.

TIPS FOR TAURUS

♉   Recognise that change is part of life.
♉   Compliment and praise others on a regular basis.

ŏ   Recognise there are people with different opinions and values.

ŏ   Don't be in a hurry to judge people.

ŏ   Every so often go somewhere you have never been before.

ŏ   Try to keep an open mind.

ŏ   Consider the advice of the air signs you meet.

YOUR GIFT TO THE WORLD

How you can make a real difference

Your special gift to the world is your capacity for love and loyalty. No other sign is as capable of enduring love. If the world were full of Taureans, the Earth world would be a beautiful fertile garden filled with loving couples all sharing in nature's bounty, a real Garden of Eden.

While you probably need to be more adaptable and understand that change is natural, your gift is to be an example of the most important and valuable thing in the world, and that's unconditional love.

SECRETS OF THE ZODIAC

FAMOUS PERSONALITIES WITH THE SUN IN TAURUS INCLUDE:

Cate Blanchett	Katharine Hepburn
Bono	Adolf Hitler
Pierce Brosnan	Glenda Jackson
Catherine the Great	Liberace
George Clooney	Shirley MacLaine
Oliver Cromwell	Dame Nellie Melba
Salvador Dali	Karl Marx
Leonardo Da Vinci	Jack Nicholson
Queen Elizabeth II	Eva Peron
Malcolm Fraser	Barbra Streisand
Sigmund Freud	Rudolph Valentino
Audrey Hepburn	Malcolm X

GEMINI

22 MAY–21 JUNE

'Be curious, not judgmental.'
GEMINI, WALT WHITMAN

YOUR LIFE MISSION

To facilitate the exchange of ideas and information.

If Aries represents the newborn infant and emerging ego, and Taurus the development of the five senses and capacity to evaluate, then Gemini is the sign where we learn to communicate. Gemini is the sign of ideas and information, where the left brain and the capacity for reason and logic are developed.

The sign of the twins is the first human sign and the sign of language, so facility with words comes naturally to you. All Geminis are highly skilled communicators. You love nothing more than absorbing, correlating and sharing information. This is your primary mission in life.

You're clever and versatile so it's easy for you to do several things at once. You crave variety and lots of mental stimulation, but you get bored easily.

You love talking to people and getting to know all about them. Your insatiable curiosity about everyone and everything means you lead an interesting life, but this constant flux and change also means you tend to skip across the surface of things. Sometimes your rapid-fire dialogue makes it difficult for people to keep up with you.

Your restlessness makes it hard for you to spend time in one place. It's the same with relationships. Other people are really important to you, but you can have trouble settling down and making a long-term commitment.

In order to do this you need to establish deeper connections that operate on an emotional level, but since you aren't really comfortable with feelings and emotions, you can find this difficult to achieve.

You crave variety and lots of mental stimulation, but you get bored easily.

And yet there is no reason why, with your mercurial temperament and the ease with which you adapt, you can't enjoy some stability and emotional support too.

Ask yourself why you aren't comfortable expressing your feelings, or why you suddenly need to run when others talk about how they feel. Can you curb your restlessness enough to stay in one place for a long time and make connections with people and places that are more durable? Are you destined to flit from one thing to the next forever, without ever finding a quiet place to rest? Is being tied down really so awful? Seeing you are so versatile, why not make the attempt to become more settled, caring and tender and express your feelings? Perhaps this is something you'd like to think about.

GIFTS FROM THE PAST

If you're a Gemini you know what Taurus is all about. You have already established a strong set of values which guide you in the world. These core values give rise to your opinions and ideas. You know what you are talking about.

Having fully integrated the core values of Taurus, you can now afford to be much more open, adaptable and flexible. You're always ready to change your point of view and are aware that there's another way of seeing things.

Whereas Taurus tends to see things from only one side,
you see things from two sides, sometimes even three,
or more.

Whereas Taureans tend to see things from only one side, you know there is more to it than that. You know everything has at least two sides—sometimes three, or even more. This duality means you are aware of both light and dark and are constantly moving between the two.

What you have already learned

- *To have a strong set of values*
- *To effectively manage your money and possessions*
- *To be practical and realistic*
- *To quickly evaluate the merit and worth of anything you encounter*
- *To be skilled in the use of your hands*
- *To be logical and rational*
- *That even the most stable and secure things in life are subject to change*
- *That being persistent doesn't always guarantee results*

ELEMENTS OF CHARACTER

Your special place in the zodiac

The third sign

Gemini is the third sign of the zodiac, the first air sign and the first human sign, the sign of the twins. Like the other air signs, Libra and Aquarius, you are a people person. None of the air signs has any animal symbolism. All are human signs, so it's human interaction and relationships that most interest you.

You're sociable, friendly and outgoing, and always looking for new information.

Mutable air

Gemini is one of the four mutable signs, all of which are adaptable and versatile, but your sign is the most restless and changeable sign of all.

This is because air is constantly on the move too. The combination of air and mutability makes you like a tornado, rapidly spinning across the surface of the land, picking things up and distributing them far and wide.

The combination of air and mutability makes you like a tornado, rapidly spinning across the surface of the land, picking things up and distributing them.

When everything is quiet and still, you are not altogether comfortable so you like to keep things moving along. You always find something to do, somewhere to go, or an interesting topic of conversation that you can share with others. It doesn't really matter who you are with, where you are going, or what you are doing, the vital thing is to keep your mind occupied and be on the move. It's the journey itself that's important.

YOUR GODS AND MYTHS

Myths, fables and legends from all parts of the world teach us that we share a common bond. The characters and events in these stories resonate with us because they contain universal symbols that we can all relate to, recognise and understand.

Storytelling comes naturally to you. Maybe you like to make up your own stories. It's just one of the many ways you like to communicate.

Mercury—Messenger of the gods

Mercury/Hermes is your chief god.[1] He rules Virgo too, so both signs are good with words and enjoy learning.

Your sign is, however, far more mercurial and mobile than Virgo, because Gemini is an air sign, whereas Virgo is stabilised by the earth element. Virgos prefer some stability, while you are constantly in motion and always looking for new experiences.

Mercury was a trickster, but he was incredibly wise too. Protector of merchants and travellers and also thieves, he is credited with inventing the alphabet, numbers, music and astronomy.

People tend to see the best in you, give you the benefit
of the doubt and forgive your transgressions.

On the day he was born Mercury invented and learned to play the lyre. The same day he stole Apollo's cows. Though he denied having taken them, Apollo suspected him right away, but Apollo was so charmed by his lyre playing that he let him keep the stolen cattle.

Mercury was generally admired for his cleverness at outwitting others. Even when he stretched the truth, he got away with it.

Some Geminis can be really cunning and even deceitful, but dark and light are always interchangeable when the trickster Mercury is about. People tend to see the best in you, give you the benefit of the doubt and forgive your transgressions.

The youthful Mercury acted as a guide, transporting souls and messages to and from the Underworld. He was the only god who could freely and safely travel to the Underworld and back. This means that you have the capacity for deep wisdom as you are able to adapt to any situation.

Though on the surface you seem to be flitting about here and there in an apparently random way, you are actually capable of going much deeper. Many Geminis are incredibly psychic and yet most are not comfortable delving too deeply into the spiritual dimension of life. This is just another of the many contradictions of your sign.

The twins—Castor and Pollux

There are many stories involving twins where one twin is good and the other is evil. To the Greeks the twins were the mortal Castor and immortal Polydeuces (more commonly called by his Roman name, Pollux) who were sons of Zeus. When Castor was killed, Pollux insisted on sharing his immortality with his brother. The twins alternated between the realm of the gods and the Underworld.

Inside many a Gemini there is both a Dr Jekyll and Mr Hyde. The task is to become aware of these opposing forces and to reconcile the two.

Because there's usually only a few minutes separating their time of birth, the horoscopes of twins are virtually identical. Because they usually share the same upbringing and parental influence, their personalities often develop in similar ways and they also share many experiences. There is often a psychic bond between twins.

> *Inside many a Gemini there is both a Dr Jekyll and Mr Hyde.*

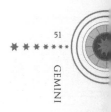

Astrological twins, those born at the same time but who are not biologically related, also have a lot in common. A few years ago I met my astrological twin and discovered that she is also an astrologer!

Whether biological twins, or cosmic twins, each soul has its own free will. We are each unique.

WHAT YOUR PLANETS REVEAL ABOUT YOU

Mercury is a small, hot world, orbiting the Sun at break-neck speed, travelling at around 30 miles per second. The closest planet to the Sun, it's aptly named for it races around the Sun in just 88 days.

Like Venus, Mercury is an inferior planet, that is, closer to the Sun than the Earth, which sets them apart from the superior planets that lie beyond Earth's orbit.

Mercury has a highly elliptical orbit, so its speed is not constant. When at perihelion (closest to the Sun) it's moving more than twice as fast as when it's aphelion (furthest from the Sun).

Now and then the planets (except the Sun and Moon) appear to move backwards, as seen from the Earth. This happens when they are making their closest approaches to the Earth. Mercury is retrograde three times each year, on each occasion for about three weeks. These are times when communication and transport problems often arise—computer problems, in particular.

Actually, Mercury retrograde is asking Geminis, and the rest of us too, to slow down our frantic pace once in a while. This is a good time for personal reflection, writing poetry or meditation. When we spend time focusing in this way rather than rushing around, we are working in harmony with this natural cycle and can then move forward with greater ease once Mercury moves direct.

Even so, there are often technical glitches and misunderstandings when the trickster planet is retrograde, which frequently happen because we have not been paying close attention.

A lot of the time Mercury is hidden in the Sun's glare, or behind the Sun itself, so just like the god, the planet Mercury is elusive.

The Gemini mind is in constant motion, just like the planet Mercury. Here one minute, gone the next. Unsettled, restless, versatile, like quicksilver, you are never still for a second.

Never more than 28 degrees away from the Sun, Mercury is always located in either the same sign as the Sun, or in the sign preceding or following.

If your Mercury is in Taurus, you probably speak more slowly than the average Gemini and are more deliberate in expressing your opinions, which would be less subject to change. Colleen McCullough and Clint Eastwood are Geminis with Mercury in Taurus.

If you have Mercury in Cancer, you are probably more softly spoken and sensitive than the average Gemini. Nicole Kidman and Venus Williams are examples of this Gemini type.

WHAT MAKES YOU TICK?

Gemini children talk and walk early. Curious about everything and anything, they are eager to explore their surroundings. Good at spelling and grammar, as a child you no doubt enjoyed puzzles and games. You probably still enjoy playing Scrabble and Trivial Pursuit.

Though you're highly intelligent, your grades at school may not have been as good as they could have been. Geminis find learning easy, but are easily distracted. While the teacher is busy keeping order in the classroom and helping the slower students, Gemini kids have already grasped the essentials and are eager to move on to the next lesson.

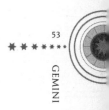

*The duality and changeable nature of Gemini makes
you hard to pin down.*

Mischief-makers one and all, the typical Gemini child likes to play pranks on their classmates, has a short attention span and a tendency to fidget. It's true that the devil finds work for idle hands, especially Gemini hands.

The duality and changeable nature of your sign makes you hard to pin down, but even so it's pretty easy to spot a Gemini. The first thing people notice about you is that you are always talking. The Gemini tongue is in constant motion, just like everything else about you.

*Many Geminis are actually twins. Multiple births seem
to be more common in June.*

The chatterbox of the zodiac, you're constantly on the lookout for new information and people to talk to. You're alert and shrewd, but your restlessness makes it difficult for you to commit to anything for long periods. Every aspect of life is coloured by your need for mental stimulation and variety, including relationships, jobs and living arrangements.

You like to keep up-to-date and always have the latest gadgets, especially computer software and mobile phones.

It comes as no surprise that your phone bills take up a large chunk of your income. If you're the parent of a Gemini teenager, or worse, Gemini twins, heaven help you.

Many Geminis are actually twins. Multiple births seem to be more common in June, and Gemini women often have twins.

Regardless of whether you are a twin or not, Geminis can have issues with their siblings. For example, you or one of your brothers or sisters might be the black sheep of the family. Perhaps one child is favoured by parents, or by fortune, while the other carries the family shadow. Not that you dwell on these things. The present fascinates you far more than wading through the emotional quagmire of the past. Geminis aren't interested in laying blame, they just accept things as they are and get on with life.

You like to keep up-to-date and always have the latest gadgets, especially computer software and mobile phones.

Keeping busy is vital. You enjoy problem-solving, and can effectively manage routine procedures too, so long as the work is interesting. You're good at dealing with details and enjoy undertaking several tasks at once.

Many Geminis work in the media and just as many are found in IT and public relations. Geminis also make good salespeople, actors, advertising executives, teachers, copywriters, translators—indeed any field where communication is the key. But being stuck behind a desk is probably not your idea of fun. There has to be movement, variety and people. As you like to keep informed about what is going on in the world too, you might become interested in politics, for you enjoy talking to people and travelling— but you're probably more interested in debating the issues than in politics as a career.

Geminis, like Librans, are the swinging voters of the world. I know one Gemini who used to be a union delegate and staunchly left-wing, but is now just as far to the political right as he was to the left.

*Gemini men are perhaps the only men in the zodiac
who have the ability to multi-task.*

Politicians often make promises that you know they are unlikely to keep. You have a large dose of healthy scepticism. There is no political trick they can come up with that hasn't already crossed your mind.

Sir Arthur Conan Doyle, creator of Sherlock Holmes, was a true multi-talented Gemini. Sherlock Holmes was the epitome of cleverness, yet Holmes had a dark side, an opium habit. When he had no interesting cases to occupy his mind, Holmes would turn to drugs. But as soon as a particularly intriguing case came along, that only he had the brain power to solve, he would then quickly change and become incredibly animated and intensely focused. As with Sherlock Holmes, the only real problem for Geminis is boredom. A most remarkable man himself, Sir Arthur Conan Doyle was a doctor and spent a lot of time campaigning for justice on a variety of human rights issues. True to the nature of air to evolve towards water, later in life Doyle developed a keen interest in spiritualism.

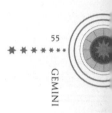

Whatever your political persuasion, you enjoy a good debate. It's fun. Because you see everything from two sides, you really don't mind which side you are on. In fact, you can even switch from one side to the other in mid-sentence.

Day and night your mind is always active, which means you can be prone to insomnia. It can be difficult to switch off the internal chatter. Reading before bedtime might help. Some Geminis are real night owls; if not out and about on the town, they sit up watching late night television or the latest movie release. Many Geminis have extensive collections of both music and film.

The typical Gemini has a quite a few hobbies. One Gemini I know likes to collect newspaper clippings on a range of topics that interest him. He also collects computer magazines, movie posters, stamps, old advertising signs, corks, postcards, keys, coasters, matches, and even plastic bread ties. Why? I'm not sure, but these things are apparently very interesting.

While Cancerians keep things for sentimental reasons, or because of their historical significance, and Taureans collect objects for their intrinsic value or as an investment, collecting ephemera seems to be more common among Geminis.

Not that you sit around the house all day navel-gazing. Sharing your pastimes with other people is part of the fun, so you enjoy swap meets, clubs and other social gatherings.

You prefer intellectual companionship over intimacy, but as you get older you might start to feel you have missed out on something. Notice I said 'feel'. Yes, you do have feelings, everyone does. It's just that you don't really understand feelings and emotions.

Though people don't usually turn to you in an emotional crisis, when they do they are often surprised to find that you understand what they are going through, and are able to offer practical advice too.

Your keen perception and friendliness means you are always willing to discuss your views openly and listen to others. Your ability to put yourself in another's shoes is a unique gift.

No doubt you have lots of friends of both sexes. Geminis seem able to relate to the opposite sex in ways that no other sign can. Gemini men are the only men in the zodiac who have the ability to multi-task, which is perhaps why Gemini men often have lots of female friends.

Your ability to put yourself in another's shoes is a unique gift.

Acknowledging your own feelings is more difficult, but eventually there comes a point when you surely must want to establish deeper connections with others by sharing your feelings.

As you reach mid-life you might sense that a piece of the puzzle has been skipped over. It isn't information that's lacking, for no one has a better grasp of facts and details than you, rather it's your feelings that you will begin to wonder about. Though your head will always rule your heart, as you get older you might find yourself becoming more emotional, sensitive and sentimental. You might even become nostalgic about the past and start to reveal your tender, kind-hearted side.

All through life you will probably retain your youthful appearance and mental alertness, keeping busy and active well into old age.

You manage stress and change better than most, though nervous disorders and respiratory problems are common Gemini ailments. These can be made worse by suppressing your emotions. Maybe it would help if you just slowed things down now and then, learned to relax and open your heart a little. Then you'll begin to unite the two sides of your twin-selves and find wholeness.

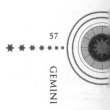

THE REALLY IMPORTANT THINGS IN YOUR LIFE

A good education

Your insatiable curiosity means you enjoy reading, study and all forms of learning. Having information at hand is critically important to you.

All Geminis take to schooling with gusto. When you are interested in a topic, you become engrossed, at least until the next really interesting thing comes along.

Whether short stories, letters to the editor, poetry or keeping a diary, writing comes naturally to you.

At school you probably enjoyed being on the debating team. No doubt you excelled at writing essays, English, languages and maths, in fact any subject you turned your attention to.

Whether short stories, letters to the editor, poetry, or keeping a diary, writing comes naturally to you. One day you might even write a bestseller. It's probably true to say that every Gemini has at least one good book in them.

A good education and the ability to communicate effectively are vital, not only to get on in the world, but these are the foundation blocks of your self-esteem. You know that a good education is the most important asset one can have.

> *It's probably true to say that every Gemini has a good book in them.*

Some Geminis have a string of qualifications after their name and, never content with what they have already achieved academically, are always seeking out new avenues of study; but most Geminis prefer to learn from life experience rather than in the classroom.

Though you share Mercury as a ruling planet with Virgo, there are a number of important differences between you. For one thing Virgo is a yin sign, while you are yang.

When Virgos want to know something, they look it up in an encyclopedia, go to the library, or do research on the web, but not you. Your first port of call is usually a friend, a neighbour, or the local shopkeeper, anyone in fact who you can talk to there and then. While Virgos turn inward for answers, you turn to other people.

Not that you aren't into books and computers too; actually, computers are ruled by Gemini. In fact your mind is just like a computer; full of facts and data, constantly changing all the time as new information and technology rapidly advances.

You're alert, inventive and often have great original ideas.

You understand that it is through people—via social contact with friends and acquaintances—that information is shared and real knowledge obtained. Life experience is the real teacher and your aim is not just to gather and absorb information, it's to share it.

Though getting a good education is vital, your chief mission is to facilitate the exchange of information and ideas, not just to acquire knowledge for its own sake.

SHARING YOUR KNOWLEDGE

How you get along with others

People you can teach:	Earth signs—Taurus, Virgo, Capricorn
Compatible similar signs:	Air signs—Gemini, Libra, Aquarius
Compatible complementary signs:	Fire signs—Aries, Leo, Sagittarius
People you can learn from:	Water signs—Cancer, Scorpio, Pisces

Relating to earth signs (Taurus, Virgo, Capricorn)

Air signs follow earth signs, so you agree with their logical and practical way of seeing the world, but you are much more outgoing and wish they would be more active and lively, like you. So you invite them to trivia nights, help them with their computer problems and suggest lots of interesting things you can do together in an attempt to help improve their lives.

But Taurus, Virgo and Capricorn can be rather anti-social, which frustrates you no end. Earth signs prefer to work things out on their own. Even so, you understand where they are coming from and are generous towards them because you want them to develop the life skills they lack.

Simple conversations can easily escalate into a war of words.

Though you share Mercury as a ruling planet with Virgo, and therefore enjoy lively discussions with them, the Gemini/Virgo relationship is one of the more difficult combinations. Simple conversations can easily escalate into a war of words as you try to show them that you are right and they are wrong.

Relating to air signs (Gemini, Libra, Aquarius)

Air signs love a good chat. Topics of conversation include current affairs, the latest trends, gossip, technology, politics, gadgets, and the newest DVD release. Air is the most social and extrovert of all the elements.

Librans, Aquarians and other Geminis are a good match for you because these people understand your duality better than most.

But since we all tend to stick with what we know and do best, the air/air relationship, while fun, comfortable and happy, does not lend itself to personal growth as much as relationships with other elements.

Relating to fire signs (Aries, Leo, Sagittarius)

Relationships with fire signs are the best match for you. Fire is spontaneous and outgoing like you, but they are right-brained, which means there are enough differences between you to keep life interesting. You can learn from one another while also respecting each others' differences. Aries and Leo are your most compatible signs; Sagittarius less so, as it's your opposite sign.

Relationships with Sagittarians are challenging because you are left-brained while they are right-brained and this is amplified by the opposition between your signs. While you focus on details, Sagittarians are more interested in the big picture. You see the trees, while Sagittarians see the forest. Though you are both adaptable and flexible, and you might be strangely attracted to one other, you can have real difficulty understanding their reasoning, and they likewise find you incomprehensible.

Relating to water signs (Cancer, Scorpio, Pisces)

Air/Water is the most challenging combination of elements. Water signs drive you crazy; you simply don't understand them on any level. Their values and thought processes seem to defy any kind of logical or reasonable explanation, and yet despite this they somehow manage to get things right, which you find frustrating and baffling in the extreme.

Water signs bypass logic and instead use instinct and intuition. To your way of thinking these are inferior and highly questionable methods of assessment. But water comes after air and therefore water signs are actually wiser than you think. You can learn a great deal from these peculiar people, if only you would let them show you.

> *When it comes to emotional intelligence, water signs are light years ahead of you.*

The Cancerians, Scorpios and Pisceans of the world would like you to be more sensitive, compassionate and spiritual, and understand the value of feelings and intuition, but they are not active/yang signs like you, they are yin and therefore they don't go out of their way to help you evolve. If it seems almost as though they are waiting for you to catch on, they are.

When it comes to emotional intelligence, water signs are light years ahead of you. Never fear, help is at hand, for if you let them, they will fill your heart with love and magic and teach you what you need to learn.

WHAT YOU NEED TO LEARN

To be comfortable with your feelings

You are just so restless that no sooner do you arrive somewhere than you want to get up and go again. Why is it that you can never sit still for more than two seconds? What you need to learn is to feel comfortable wherever you are, but you are always jumping up and dashing off, always seeking something new.

*When you're faced with emotions you feel like you have
swallowed something the wrong way.*

To be comfortable with your feelings, just like Hermes/Mercury, you need to dive down into the Underworld now and then.

To do this you need to face your feelings, but doing that makes you nervous and uncomfortable, it's not a place you like to go. Emotions are not rational and anything that can't be explained rationally is scary to you.

Water signs have a deep level of emotional understanding and they want you to acknowledge the value of being sensitive. They are attuned to these more subtle vibrations. But when you're faced with emotions you feel like you have swallowed something the wrong way. You can even start to feel like you are choking.

In order to truly connect with people on a deeper soul level, you need to be able to talk about your feelings, but you are much more at ease with your ideas. Water signs can show you that there is another way.

*Why is it that you can never sit still for more than
two seconds?*

But even when you ask water signs a direct question, you don't get a response you can understand. They might as well be speaking a foreign language. You are so good at languages and words, surely what they say and what they do must be comprehensible. Yet it simply does not make any sense! It drives you crazy. What are they on about?

The trouble is that feelings cannot be explained logically. You think anything associated with the unconscious, including the people who understand this dimension, are slow and dense, when in actual fact they are just taking the time to understand how they feel.

Learning to be comfortable with how you feel might seem impossible, but Cancerians and the other water signs can help you to do this. All you have to do is listen and learn, and you're good at that already.

SECRETS OF THE ZODIAC

TAKING THE NEXT STEP

Water signs are caring, sympathetic people who want to understand what lies beneath the surface. You, on the other hand, want to skip across the surface and cover as much territory as possible. The difference is that you seek quantity, while they seek quality.

You are in such a hurry, you don't have the time to spend in one place. You think, why bother? What is the point?

Yet wouldn't it be nice to rest awhile and be comfortable in one place, just take a deep breath, sit still and relax?

Wouldn't it be nice to rest awhile and be comfortable in one place, just take a deep breath, sit still and relax?

Putting down roots is a tricky business for you too. Domestic stability and a secure home life are associated with Cancer, the sign which follows Gemini, so in order to get there you first need to connect with others emotionally, or at least to be open to the concept. Cancerians can show you how to feel comfortable no matter where you are.

The first thing you need to do is to just slow down.

Over the course of your lifetime you have numerous opportunities to learn how to do this. Every four months or so, when Mercury retrogrades, you can connect more deeply to others. These are times when you can get in touch your feelings more easily.

Water signs can teach you about the magic that resides in dreams, in music and in art. Cancerians, Scorpios and Pisceans can also teach you compassion and understanding and how to have deeper access to your imagination.

When you look at a picture of the Moon and one of Mercury, you'll see that they are actually very similar. They are about the same size too. So you share with Cancerians a special relationship that comes from understanding the changeable nature of life.

You both have the ability to adapt, to wax and wane. Cancerians understand your duality; in fact no one understands you better. There is a Gemini or two deep within them, for they have already learned what you are now learning.

Though you find it quite disconcerting, realise that water signs can teach you how to go deeper and find wisdom. Remember, this is really where Hermes/Mercury wants to take you.

TIPS FOR GEMINI

II   When you arrive somewhere, just sit down and relax.
II   Learn how to meditate.
II   Every so often think about how you are feeling.
II   As an experiment try to talk more slowly and see how it feels.
II   Recognise that talking is only one form of communication.
II   Keep a dream journal.
II   Consider the advice of the water signs you meet.

YOUR GIFT TO THE WORLD

How you can make a real difference

Your unique gift to the world is your ability to communicate with anyone. No matter who they are, you can put yourself in their shoes. Regardless of their creed, religion, nationality, political persuasion or sexual orientation, you just tell it like it is; you hold no prejudices against anyone. You are completely impartial. You can adapt to any circumstance, adjust to any situation and get along with everyone, anywhere, anytime. Yours is the most open-minded and approachable sign of the zodiac. If the world were only populated by Geminis, there would never be any communication problems—though the phone lines would be continually jammed.

FAMOUS PERSONALITIES WITH THE SUN IN GEMINI INCLUDE:

Annette Bening

Johnny Depp

Arthur Conan Doyle

Bob Dylan

Clint Eastwood

Errol Flynn

Michael J. Fox

Anne Frank

Judy Garland

Che Guevara

Morgan Freeman

Helen Hunt

Angelina Jolie

Tom Jones

JFK

Nicole Kidman

Michael Leunig

Kylie Minogue

Marilyn Monroe

Mike Myers

The Olsen Twins

Salman Rushdie

Jean-Paul Sartre

Walt Whitman

CANCER

22 JUNE–23 JULY

'Our prime purpose in this life is to help others.
And if you can't help them, at least don't
hurt them.'

CANCER, DALAI LAMA (14TH)

YOUR LIFE MISSION

To find emotional security by forming attachments. To have a place to call home where you feel protected.

Cancer is the first water sign. As the water element is related to feelings and emotions, you are a caring, sensitive person who shows consideration towards others. Kind and responsive, you're a tender-hearted soul and just like a real crab, you have a tough shell designed to protect you from the outside world.

Your imagination and intuition are equally well developed so you have a great talent for sensing what is just around the corner. These instincts guide you through life and you rely on them absolutely.

Resourceful and tenacious, you know what you want from life, but you don't always take the most direct route. You're ambitious, but you wait for the right moment before you act. In all you do, it's important you feel comfortable and secure before you proceed. The ambience must be just right.

When the atmosphere and circumstances are most conducive, your confidence grows and then you feel more able to cope with the slings and arrows of life. You are prepared and feel protected.

Your imagination and intuition are equally well developed and you have a great talent for sensing what is just around the corner.

Feeling an inward sense of support is of paramount importance to you. It gives you a secure base from which you can proceed. This is also why home and family are important for your sign; they make you feel secure.

Even so, now and then you can still feel insecure, especially when you find yourself in the spotlight, for basically you are shy. You like to keep part of yourself hidden from the world. Privacy is important to you; in fact,

it's just as important as security, but as you also have a strong need to make your mark in the world, you are faced with a dilemma.

For how can you maintain your privacy and feel secure while being out there in the world striving towards your goals? As you become more successful in life, how do you manage that uncomfortable feeling of being exposed and vulnerable? Does being noticed mean you have to sacrifice your privacy? And as you take on more responsibilities, how do you make the time to retreat into your shell now and then so you still feel protected? Are these things mutually exclusive?

How can you stay true to yourself, honour your natural sensitivity, find emotional security and at the same time follow your heart's desire towards your goals? Does it all depend on the mood of the moment and cycle of the Moon?

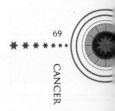

GIFTS FROM THE PAST

If you are born under the sign of Cancer it means you have inherited a lifetime of Gemini wisdom. You know how to communicate effectively and have a natural ease with words and language.

As a Cancerian you now have the opportunity to develop and express your imagination and intuition.

What you have already learned

- *To generate and communicate original ideas*
- *To be aware and perceptive*
- *The art of conversation*
- *To develop the left side of your brain*
- *To be sociable and friendly*
- *To adapt to your surroundings*
- *To be versatile and flexible*
- *That there are two sides to everything*

ELEMENTS OF CHARACTER

Your special place in the zodiac

The fourth sign

Cancer is the fourth sign of the zodiac. The fourth sign corresponds with the fourth house, which is the zone of the sky directly below the Earth. It's another reason why having a home and a feeling of security is of paramount importance to you. Once this area of your life is set, you can build from there.

Your crab shell that travels with you at all times is like a rudder, helping you to navigate the waves and currents of life.

The number four is also associated with form and structure which is why you strive for both material and emotional security.

Before you begin building a home you need a plan, a suitable location and the resources to do so. These are fundamental principles by which you live your life.

Cardinal water

Cancer is a cardinal sign, and all cardinal signs are natural leaders; however, you are not as direct or forceful in your leadership style as the other cardinal signs.

Cardinal energy is outwardly directed, while water flows and moves and is shaped by the surrounding environment. The combination of water and cardinal energy makes you move like a river, sometimes flowing slowly, sometimes fast, all the while twisting and turning, heading towards the sea. Your crab shell that travels with you at all times is like a rudder helping you to navigate the waves and currents of life.

YOUR GODS AND MYTHS

Your sign has not always been a crab. The Egyptians knew Cancer as the sign of the scarab, or dung beetle, a symbol of fertility, life, death and rebirth. Many ancient cultures saw Cancer as the gateway through which souls incarnated on Earth and the place to which they returned after death.

The Sun enters Cancer at the beginning of summer (northern hemisphere), the longest day of the year, a time of abundance and fertility. Yet at the summer solstice, daylight hours begin to shorten and we start the retreat towards winter. No matter where you live, or travel, you know that in order to move forward in life it's sometimes necessary to retreat.

No matter where you live, you know that in order
to move forward in life it's sometimes necessary
to retreat.

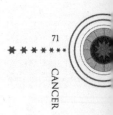

Cancer is a yin, or feminine sign, and the Moon, your ruling planet is the main feminine archetype. In fact there are a number of important goddesses connected with your sign.

Juno—Goddess of marriage

Juno/Hera was the long-suffering wife of Jupiter/Zeus. She is the archetypal power behind the throne. Sometimes taken for granted by her husband, she nonetheless wielded considerable influence. She is the goddess of marriage and commitment. For those who identify with this goddess, relationships come first. Marriage is seen as a life-long commitment and a sacred oath.

It was Hera who awarded the crab its place in the zodiac. She honoured the crab when it nipped Heracles on the toe while he was fighting the Hydra.

Ceres—Mother goddess of fertility

Ceres/Demeter[1] was the goddess of fertility. She is the traditional mother archetype. She's compassionate and caring and is also associated with Virgo as the goddess of the harvest.

She had such a powerful maternal instinct that when her daughter Persephone was abducted by Hades and taken to the Underworld, her grief stopped the crops from growing. This goddess represents the part of you that needs to protect and care for others, especially your family.

Lots of astrology books say that Cancerian women are only interested in marriage and having babies, but this isn't true.

Those who identify strongly with Ceres make good parents, but can be overprotective and have difficulty allowing their children freedom for fear they will come to harm. Cancerian parents can find it hard to let go of their children.

Mother is a powerful figure. Our personal development depends to a large extent on the quality of the parenting we receive.

Those with a strong Moon or Cancerian influence sometimes seek out a mother or father figure who can provide the protection and security they need. Likewise, they may 'mother' their friends or their partner.

Diana—Goddess of the hunt

Lots of astrology books say that Cancerian women are only interested in marriage and having babies, but this isn't true. Some Cancerian women love the idea of having a large family, and take to motherhood with relative ease, but there are others who have no maternal instinct whatsoever.

While some Cancerian women identify with Ceres, just as many identify with Diana/Artemis.

Diana was the lunar goddess of childbirth and hunting. When she was born she helped her mother give birth to her twin brother Apollo (the Sun), acting as midwife.

> *Diana/Artemis was a virgin goddess, so there's part of you that wants to remain free to pursue your own interests.*

Although associated with childbirth and motherhood, Diana was a virgin goddess, so there's part of you that wants to remain free to pursue your own interests.

Artemis carried a bow and arrow and had hounds as her hunting companions. She went after what she wanted and was highly independent.

Artemis women usually love animals, especially dogs, and many can be found working as counsellors, therapists, nurses and in other healing professions.

Cancerian women, and/or those with a strong Moon in their birth charts, genuinely care about the welfare of others, but those who identify strongly with Diana are often not that interested in motherhood.

Just as Artemis came to the aid of her mother on several occasions, Cancerians sometimes take on the role of looking after a parent, sometimes from an early age; and this can be the reason why they choose not to enter into parenthood as adults.

Actually, children are astrologically associated with Leo, the sign after Cancer. So Cancerians recognise the importance of having a secure home environment before bringing children into the world, and many opt to start a family later in life. You take the role seriously, understand the responsibility involved and are happy to wait until you have established yourself and found some security.

Even so, a surprising number of Cancerian women choose not to have children at all. Motherhood is simply not on their 'to do' list.

CANCER

WHAT YOUR PLANETS REVEAL ABOUT YOU

Astrologically the Moon is just as important as the Sun. This is because from Earth the Sun and Moon appear almost identical in size, which, when you think about it, is really quite amazing.

When the Sun, Earth and Moon align perfectly, the result is an eclipse. Every year there are at least two solar and two lunar eclipses. Solar eclipses occur at New Moon, when the Moon moves in front of the Sun; while lunar eclipses happen at Full Moon when the Moon moves through the Earth's shadow.

Though historically eclipses have been viewed as evil omens, this is not so much the case today. Nevertheless, the new moon, full moon and especially eclipses are potent alignments that Cancerians in particular seem to respond to.

The Moon is the closest body to the Earth; we can even see it in broad daylight, so you often feel overexposed and consequently quite vulnerable.

While the planets are revolving around the Sun, the Moon is first orbiting the Earth, so you have a unique perspective, unlike any other sign of the zodiac.

Sometimes the Moon reveals its full face, at other times it's only partly visible, and sometimes it's completely invisible. It all depends on the phase of the Moon, which is determined by its position relative to the Sun and the Earth. This means that you are easily influenced by subtle fluctuations in your environment and people's emotions.

Just like the cycle of the Moon, you wax and wane.

The Moon spins on its axis once a month, but always shows the same face to the Earth.

The Moon is the closest body to the Earth; we can even see it in broad daylight, so you often feel overexposed and consequently quite vulnerable.

Just like we never see the far side of the Moon, there's a side of you which is intensely private; a part of yourself you never reveal to others no matter what the Moon phase, or how close you are to others.

We never see the far side of the Moon, and there's a side of you which is intensely private too; a part of yourself you never reveal to others no matter what the Moon phase, or how close you are to others.

The Moon landing took place on 20 July 1969[2] when the Sun was in Cancer, the sign ruled by the Moon. When Neil Armstrong stepped onto the Moon, it was a Monday in many parts of the world, the day of the week named for the Moon. Synchronistically, the glyph for Cancer ♋ looks just like 69, only turned on its side.

WHAT MAKES YOU TICK?

When we are born the first person we meet is our mother and she makes a big impression. The quality of mothering we receive has a major influence on our development, in particular on our ability to form emotional attachments.

Whatever our upbringing, or astrological influences, we look for connections that are familiar to us, for they are reminiscent of our early home life, even if our childhood was traumatic. Because of your innate sensitivity, early childhood influences are perhaps even more profound.

*Though it is not always apparent to others, yours is one
of the most ambitious signs of the zodiac.*

Just as every month the Moon returns to the position it occupied at birth, we expect our mothers to be there for us—but she can't be there all the time, and even if she is, that too can cause problems and make it more difficult to separate later on.

Cancerian children like to feel snug and secure and love being read to at bedtime. Listening to fairytales is both comforting and helps to inspire their active imaginations.

Whether it's a security blanket, a dummy, a favourite soft toy, or their pet rabbit, emotional connections make these kids feel safe. Those crab claws hold on tightly. It can be tough when the time comes to let go.

If you bond too tightly—be it to your mother, your children or your partner—you can find it difficult to let go, which you need to do in order to establish your own identity and independence. Getting the mix right is one of your main challenges in life.

You're sentimental about mementos and other family heirlooms and have a deep appreciation for family heritage and tradition. Whether you are interested in researching your family tree or the wider scope of history, or both, lots of Cancerians are fascinated by the past.

*Though it can be difficult to explain your reasoning
or feelings to others, as it's mostly unconscious, your
intuition seldom leads you astray.*

Family, marriage and parenting can take on epic proportions for some Cancerians. King Edward VIII, for example, chose to give up his throne so he could marry Wallis Simpson, the Duchess of Windsor, and Princess Diana's relationship problems were front-page headlines around the globe. King Henry VIII was another Cancerian royal with some relationship issues.

Of course, not every Cancerian is in the public eye, but this is often part of the problem because you really do need your privacy.

For Cancerian royalty the problem is compounded because royalty is traditionally associated with Leo, the sign which comes after yours, so chances are that none of these people were really comfortable in the spotlight. Let's hope Prince William has an easier time of it.

Princess Diana shared her name with the goddess of the hunt. Ironically, it was she who was the prey, pursued relentlessly by the paparazzi throughout her life. Her first child, Prince William, was born on the summer solstice, 21 June 1982, which was also the day of a solar eclipse, so he has both the Sun and Moon in Cancer. Children are often born with the same Sun sign or Moon sign as their parents and often inherit other planetary influences as well.

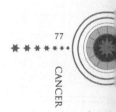

When a relationship ends, you can be unwilling to let go completely. If you can, you like to stay friends. You have a forgiving nature and a kind heart.

Hostile, aggressive or noisy people can make you retreat into your shell, but when you feel angry yourself, it's important to let it out.

You are so in tune with your feelings that you know immediately when something is amiss, though sometimes you have no idea why you are reacting the way you are. Even if you can't exactly pinpoint what's bothering you, you still feel it, and respond accordingly.

Because you often feel vulnerable, sometimes you try to hide your emotions, but they have a way of seeping out. You cry at sad movies, or when touched by someone's generosity, and sometimes just because you need an emotional release. You might explode angrily and quite unexpectedly, and the next moment you can be the life of the party, so much so, that you almost seem like a Leo.

No two Cancerians are alike. A great deal depends on the position of the Moon, your ruling planet.

Hostile, aggressive or noisy people can make you retreat into your shell.

Tom Cruise, for example, has his Moon in Leo, so he is quite happy taking centre stage. Nelson Mandela has his Moon in Scorpio, so he has a deep capacity for understanding born of suffering. Princess Diana's Moon was in Aquarius, which made her interested in humanitarian causes and also subject to emotional fluctuations.

You're highly aware of the subtle energies and vibrations that most people are unable to perceive. You sense when people or animals are suffering and are often deeply affected by this suffering.

Though it can be difficult to explain your reasoning or feelings to others, as it's mostly unconscious, you are always guided by your intuition and it seldom leads you astray. You simply cannot ignore your inner voice, nor should you. It's not just women's intuition, Cancerian men have it too.

Though it's not always apparent to others, yours is one of the most ambitious signs of the zodiac. Others may underestimate your strength and tenacity and think you are a real softy, which of course you are, but you're also highly driven and incredibly determined.

Cancerians can be found working as writers, researchers, real estate agents or veterinarians, or in the health and healing/welfare sector, but always in an ambient environment, where management really cares about its staff and respects the needs of family is a high priority. Cancerians are equally happy working behind the scenes or in positions of authority.

Some Cancerians choose to be full-time carers or parents and many can be found working from home. In fact, by starting your own home-based business you can really find your true niche in life.

This is a creative option which allows you the freedom to follow your ambitions, fulfil your need for security and privacy, while also caring for your family, and/or pets. Better still, if you work from home you can manage both domestic and professional responsibilities as the mood takes you.

You probably enjoy cooking, homemaking, dinner parties, renovating, and all kinds of domestic activities including gardening and do-it-yourself courses in home improvement.

Whatever face you show the world, there is a large part of you that remains an enigma. Like the changing face of the Moon you are bright and glowing and full one day, quiet, hidden, dark and intense the next, and every phase in between.

You simply cannot ignore your inner voice, nor should you.

There remains within you a secret self that very few people are ever privileged to see.

Your life may take a few twists and turns, like a meandering river, but along the way you're learning to navigate your own course towards your ultimate destiny.

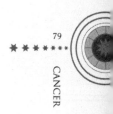

THE REALLY IMPORTANT THINGS IN YOUR LIFE

A place to call home

Crabs are amphibious, so you can survive in different environments and, like real crabs, you carry your home—your protective shell—wherever you go.

Having a home is a primary need for all Cancerians. When life gets tough, you can retreat into your shell and bury yourself under the sand. Here you feel safe, secure and protected. Soon you emerge, with your energy restored, feeling refreshed, buoyant and renewed.

Leaving the parental home can be a daunting process, indeed a giant leap for many Cancerians, but it's an important step because you need to establish your own home base before you can confidently and fully express your individuality and creativity.

However, in one sense home isn't really found in a specific location, it is an inner feeling of emotional security and belonging which is not necessarily tied to a place. For many Cancerians, home is where your loved ones are; be they family, friends, or pets.

Though you may feel homesick when you spend a long time away from home, in some ways it really doesn't matter where you are; Timbuktu or Xanadu, the important thing is to feel you have the emotional support you need.

Having a home of your own fulfils a very deep need within you.

Even so, having a home of your own fulfils a very deep need within you. Above all you are looking for a personal sanctuary. You have no qualms about taking on a mortgage and are keen to pay it off quickly. Most Cancerians are excellent money managers, quite canny really.

A good friend of mine decided she would buy a house on her own—no easy feat on a single income. One day she hopes to write children's books, but for now she's sticking with her secure day job. She has a long-term plan and is on track.

Though you are highly creative and imaginative, you are more security conscious. You cannot really thrive when you are in an unsupportive environment, or with insensitive people who are critical or hostile, nor when you have nowhere to turn for help.

On your journey through life you are always looking to make meaningful connections. You know when you find them, because you immediately feel right at home.

But there is no direct route, no map to follow, only your own internal compass. Since crabs walk sideways, you might take many detours before you reach your destination. When you become sidetracked you actually encounter the most interesting things which often indirectly lead you towards your eventual goal.

Part of the reason you often become sidetracked also has to do with your internal navigation system, for when it comes to getting your bearings— that is, north, south, east and west—Cancerians seem to have more trouble than most. I know three people who have this problem and they are all Cancerians. If you ask them which way is north, invariably they point south.

None of them is at all worried by not knowing which way is which, and at the end of the day it doesn't really matter. Even though you might get lost now and then, or take the occasional detour, ultimately you know exactly where you are going. Like Diana/Artemis, you are always on target.

Ultimately, that destination is Leo where you will feel more confident to express your creativity. After the midlife transition this will be easier to do, because by then you will have found the security and stability you have been looking for.

SHARING YOUR KNOWLEDGE

How you get along with others

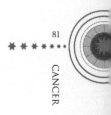

People you can teach:	Air signs—Gemini, Libra, Aquarius
Compatible similar signs:	Water signs—Cancer, Scorpio, Pisces
Compatible complementary signs:	Earth signs—Taurus, Virgo, Capricorn
People you can learn from:	Fire signs—Aries, Leo, Sagittarius

Relating to air signs (Gemini, Libra, Aquarius)

Relationships between air signs and water signs are never easy. Part of the problem is that air signs have a tendency to think that they are intellectually superior.

You make decisions according to your gut instinct.

While they are good at managing people and the day-to-day business of living, air signs often fail to understand nuance, feelings, emotions, instinct and intuition, for these things are not logical.

You make decisions according to your gut instinct and relate to other people from a deeper place, not just on a head level.

You can help air signs evolve, not by telling them what to do, but rather by example and inference.

It's your role to educate air signs about human emotion and the value of imagination and intuition but, since you are yin and they are yang, this is not an easy thing to do. Air signs are good communicators, but sometimes they just don't listen.

You understand instinctively that the way you can help them evolve is not by telling them what to do, but rather by example and inference; unfortunately much of this goes straight over the air-head.

If air signs hang around long enough, they might start to realise that your point of view and values have merit, but this will only happen if they are willing to recognise that you are much wiser than they think you are.

Relating to water signs (Cancer, Scorpio, Pisces)

You probably have a number of water sign friends. Most relationships between water signs are mutually supportive for all are sympathetic and understanding by nature. You feel comfortable sharing your most intimate and personal feelings with each other. Best of all, at the end of a long week your water sign friends can help you de-brief, relax and restore your faith in human nature.

All water signs share a sympathetic bond and similar value system.

All water signs share a sympathetic bond and similar value system and are always ready to support one another; so you can always count on these people and they know they can turn to you when in need.

Relating to earth signs (Taurus, Virgo, Capricorn)

Earth signs are great allies and they help you feel secure. Taurus is probably your best match. Virgos share your need to have time alone now and then, so they also respect your privacy. But Virgos can be a bit nitpicky and critical at times, so select a Virgo who has evolved beyond this tendency and you should be right.

Your opposite sign is Capricorn and as with all relationships between opposing signs, you can bring out the best and the worst in one another. Often what happens with the Cancer/Capricorn relationship is that they act as a kind of surrogate parent to you. They can help you attain your goals and make you feel secure, but this can lead to a dependency situation on your part. This is not always an ideal situation for an adult relationship.

Relating to fire signs (Aries, Leo, Sagittarius)

More than any other signs, fire signs will test you, but nevertheless these are the very people from whom you can learn the most.

While you are highly imaginative and creative, often you fear stepping out of your comfort zone and acting independently on your own. You can feel exposed and highly vulnerable. Encounters with fire signs can make you feel anxious, but at the same time they're willing to help you become more confident and outgoing, and they can really help you come out of your shell.

★ ★ ★ ★ ★ ★ ★

CANCER

WHAT YOU NEED TO LEARN

To find out who you really are

Leo is the sign following Cancer so what you most need is a stronger sense of your own identity. Like Pisceans, you can easily, and often unconsciously, identify so much with another person that you lose yourself.

While security is your primary goal in life, when will you feel secure enough? At some point you might start to ask yourself this question.

You think that once you attain the right level of security, you will then be free to create, but that's not what happens. You can easily become trapped in a kind of Groundhog Day experience and never get to the point where you are confident and secure enough to take the next step.

While security is your primary goal, when will you ever feel secure enough? At some point you might start to ask yourself this question.

Ultimately, yours is one of the most imaginative and creative signs of the zodiac, but you are so sensitive that it's difficult for you to put yourself 'out there'. You need to develop the confidence to take more risks and fly closer to the Sun. To do this you need to work out who you really are.

Maybe it has something to do with the fact that the Moon first revolves around the Earth, so in order to get to the Sun—where your creativity can truly shine—you must first find a secure, grounded and stable place, symbolised by the Earth. You need to develop a really deep inner sense of who you are, and this will provide the security you need.

It's an easy trap to fall into; settling for the security of having a roof over your head, a family and the relationship you thought you wanted, when all the time there is another part of you that just wants to be free to express yourself without worrying about the next mortgage payment. You are great at sensing and catering to others' needs, but what about your own?

When you let go of the familiar safety net before you feel ready, you can begin to feel anxious, so most of the time you choose the safe option, but then you never really do what you want to do. You might end up living someone else's life, not your own.

But help is at hand. There is a solution to this dilemma and it can be found in the most unlikely place.

TAKING THE NEXT STEP

What you need to realise is that you can learn how to become more confident and outgoing from the fire signs you meet, the very people who you find so annoying and bothersome. Yes, they challenge you, but in the same way that you want the air signs to understand feelings, the fire signs want you to become more independent and sure of yourself.

Once you are out of your shell, you begin to feel truly alive.

You may not realise it, but you have more in common with fire signs than you might assume. They're imaginative people too; it's just that they are more extroverted than you. They're optimistic, know who they are and what they want, and they just go for it. They don't take no for an answer. You wish you had some of their dynamic energy, but you feel wary. Can they really be as positive and successful as they appear to be? Why are they always so enthusiastic about everything? You wish you had some of their courage and assertiveness. But at the same time they are just too full-on, you feel like they are trying to sell you something and you are not sure you want to buy.

It's like that recurring dream where you have to go on stage and can't remember your lines, or worse, you find yourself standing there stark naked!

Fire signs, especially Leos, can be so self-centred and egocentric they only seem interested in themselves. Sure, they are happy most of time, who wouldn't be when you only have to think about your own needs? They are used to be being in the limelight, but being the centre of attention bothers you for you are likely to get stage fright.

CANCER

That's why you hold yourself back and why it's difficult to perform. What if you don't feel like it? What if you commit to something and then are not prepared when the time comes? What if you wake up that day and don't feel like facing the world? What then? You don't want to let people down, but what if you don't feel up to it?

It's like that recurring dream where you have to go on stage and can't remember your lines, or worse, find yourself standing there stark naked!

Fire signs don't worry about these things; they just get up and go. Best of all they're eager to help you do likewise.

When you're feeling sad, anxious or fearful, or any other emotion that holds you back, it's the fire signs who can turn these feelings into positive emotions, like joy and bliss, by showing you how to take hold of life's opportunities.

Aries people have leadership qualities like you, but they have incredible courage and assertiveness and never hesitate to take action. They can teach you how to be more direct.

Sagittarians are happy-go-lucky free spirits who love to travel, never get homesick and always look on the bright side. They can teach you to be more enthusiastic and to have faith that everything will turn out for the best.

Because they are keen for you to be more like them, fire signs go out of their way to encourage you, often pushing you forward, even when you don't feel ready. This causes you a great deal of stress, but at the same time you know, being the highly intuitive being that you are, that there is some merit in what they are trying to do. Once you are out of your shell, you begin to feel truly alive. You feel like a weight has been lifted.

Every sign struggles to come to terms with the sign following their Sun sign, in your case this is Leo, the sign ruled by the Sun itself. This is where you have a bit of a blind spot, and let's face it, the Sun can be truly blinding. The Moon has no light of its own; it only reflects the light of the Sun.

In the same way, Leos help you see yourself more clearly. The Sun might be big and hot and dazzling, but it's also beautiful and radiant and filled with creative energy, just like you. When you accept their guidance and bask in their reflected light, then you reach your fullest potential and rise up, silvery and glowing like a beautiful full moon.

TIPS FOR CANCER

- Just do it.
- When you are feeling down, make an effort to look on the bright side.
- Do something creative on a regular basis.
- Be happy, joyful and optimistic.
- Spend some time with children now and then.
- Find a balance between give and take.
- Consider the advice of the fire signs you meet.

YOUR GIFT TO THE WORLD

How you can make a real difference

You can make a real difference to the world because you have such a great instinct for what is needed to make people feel content and happy. Your kind and understanding heart senses when someone is in need, be it people or animals, and you don't hesitate to step in and help.

If there were only Cancerians living on planet Earth, no child would suffer, no older person would be alone and there would be no homelessness— it would just be one big happy family.

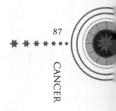

FAMOUS PERSONALITIES WITH THE SUN IN CANCER INCLUDE:

Kevin Bacon

Richard Branson

Tom Cruise

Dalai Lama (14th)

Princess Diana

Judith Durham

King Edward VIII

Harrison Ford

Tom Hanks

Ernest Hemingway

King Henry VIII

Sir Edmund Hillary

Chris Isaak

Frida Kahlo

Helen Keller

Nelson Mandela

Marcel Proust

George Orwell

Rembrandt

Barbara Stanwyck

Meryl Streep

Nikola Tesla

Gough Whitlam

Prince William

LEO

24 JULY–23 AUGUST

'There is no coming to consciousness
without pain.'
Leo, C.G. Jung

YOUR LIFE MISSION

To express yourself creatively to show and affirm who you are—a unique individual through which the creative spirit expresses itself.

As a Leo you're a highly creative person who is chiefly interested in self-expression. Your confidence is high and you are determined to follow your heart wherever it leads you. It's your role to use your creative talents to showcase your individuality, for in this way you discover and become who you truly are.

Generous and affectionate, you're a dynamic person who makes a strong impression wherever you go. You enjoy taking the lead and being in charge. Your grand plans might seem grandiose or unworkable to others, but somehow you make them happen.

To fulfil your life mission to express yourself creatively in all you undertake, you have both the energy and the persistence to carry it off.

Because you are mostly interested in your creative output and the vision which inspires it, you are not that focused on the small details. You tend to assume they will take care of themselves, but unfortunately they don't. Most of the time, you prefer to delegate the small stuff, while you supervise. Sometimes you just assume that the details will fall into place by themselves, or maybe you don't even notice them until they are big enough to cause problems, which is when life can become difficult.

Just when you are nearing the finish line and starting to think about your next big project, an irritating small insect starts buzzing around your head. It even has the temerity to land on you, or on top of your magnificent creation and spoil the whole effect.

In all you undertake you have both the energy and the persistence to carry it off.

While you relish a challenge, and thrive on competition, nothing frustrates you more than those last-minute details that someone has forgotten to deal with.

But hang on a moment…isn't this your show? Aren't you the one who's in charge? Isn't it up to you to see things through to the end, and doesn't that include managing the small stuff?

You're much happier when you can leave the details to someone else, but when you do, you're no longer in charge any more; someone else has taken over and that's just not on.

But how can you stay focused on your grand vision if you have to attend to the small stuff yourself? Is it possible to be the king of all you survey, including the tiny insects?

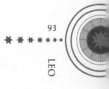

GIFTS FROM THE PAST

If you are a Leo it means you have inherited a lifetime of Cancerian wisdom. You know that family support is everything. Most Leos have a feeling of inner security which generates confidence. Many Leos come from well-to-do families, but whatever your upbringing you rarely feel insecure, because deep down you know who you are.

You want to express yourself creatively as an independent and unique individual, but ultimately you know you can rely on your family for protection and support in times of difficulty. Even if your family is not in a position to help you, you still feel that somehow everything will turn out for the best. You instinctively feel that you will be able to find the support in life that you need, when you need it.

What you have already learned

- *The importance of tradition*
- *To follow your heart*
- *That family is important*

- *To be guided by your feelings and instincts*
- *To feel you belong*
- *To nurture others*
- *To honour your parents*
- *To feel secure*

ELEMENTS OF CHARACTER

Your special place in the zodiac

The fifth sign

Leo is the fifth sign of the zodiac and the second fire sign. Before Leo there are four signs, one of each element; like four legs of a solid throne upon which you sit, they add to your feeling of being secure and stable. You have already learned a great deal: Aries gave you drive and energy; Taurus taught you how to be persistent and evaluate; Gemini gave you the ability to communicate; and Cancer taught you to trust your instincts and express your feelings.

You want to create something that truly showcases your special talents and which authentically represents who you are.

Consequently, you've developed a strong sense of self. Now you want to create something that showcases your special talents and which authentically represents who you are.

Fixed fire

The Sun is in Leo at the hottest time of the year so it makes sense that the Sun is your ruling planet. Fixed fire is like an eternal flame that burns

SECRETS OF THE ZODIAC

steady and strong, with endless fuel, like the Sun itself. You radiate warmth, have a sunny outlook and have lots of energy in reserve.

YOUR GODS AND MYTHS

The Sun symbolises consciousness. At its highest level, this makes you interested in expanding your conscious awareness.

With the Sun in Leo, you must be true to yourself and honour your core essential nature. As you become more conscious this sparks new creative ideas which you express, which in turn leads to more self-awareness.

Apollo—God of the sun

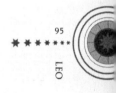

Apollo[1] was one of the most important deities in both Greece and Rome. He was the god of the Sun, light, truth, music, poetry, the arts and prophecy, and the brother of Artemis, goddess of the Moon. Apollo drove a chariot which drew the Sun across the heavens.

In one famous story, Apollo's son, Phaethon, asked his father if he could drive his chariot. Apollo told his son not to undertake such a dangerous journey as he was not yet mature enough, but Phaethon was determined. Apollo gave him a special ointment to protect him from the intense heat and advised his son how to safely manage the journey. But in his enthusiasm, Phaethon did not heed his father's advice. He went too high, too fast and too close to the Sun. Apollo watched on helplessly as his son crashed and burned.

Leo represents the maturity that comes from experience as well as the boundless enthusiasm of youth, and why it's vital to understand the difference.

There's an important lesson here for everyone, and especially for Leos. You need to learn to take instruction from others, especially when young.

Before you start driving your magnificent Sun chariot across the sky, you first need to get a licence.

Leo represents the maturity that comes from experience as well as the boundless enthusiasm of youth, and why it's vital to understand the difference, for it's true that pride often comes before a fall.

Androcles and the lion

King of the beasts and king of the jungle, from the earliest times the lion has symbolised strength and power. There are many stories involving lions and they all tell us something about you.

One of Aesop's fables tells of a Roman slave named Androcles who had escaped and was looking for food and shelter. One day he came across a ferocious-looking lion. Androcles was about to flee, but the lion didn't attack him. Instead the lion held up his paw which was swollen and bleeding with a thorn deeply embedded in it.

King of the beasts and king of the jungle, from the earliest times the lion has symbolised strength and power.

Androcles gently removed the thorn and bandaged the wound. The lion was thankful and the two became friends.

Some time later, both the lion and Androcles were captured and taken to Rome. The slave was sentenced to be thrown to the lions and the lion was starved in order to make him ravenous and aggressive.

When the day came for Androcles to be thrown to the lions, the arena was packed, the crowd eagerly awaiting the bloody spectacle, but when the lion entered the arena he recognised his friend. Instead of attacking him, he began licking his hand, like a faithful dog.

The audience was stunned and began to cheer. When the emperor heard the story, he agreed to release both Androcles and the lion.

Whatever our position in life, whether starving or wounded, or in a position of power like the emperor, this story illustrates the importance of gratitude, which ultimately sets us free.

WHAT YOUR PLANETS REVEAL ABOUT YOU

When the Sun is shining we feel good about life. We feel happy and positive and we're confident that everything will turn out for the best. Because the Sun is your ruling planet, you feel like this most of the time, even when storm clouds are gathering.

Because the Sun is at the centre of the solar system, it's natural that you should feel you are at the centre of things. You are a star! You radiate warmth and win friends wherever you go and you're always willing to share your good fortune with others. In fact your sign is the most generous sign of the zodiac.

It seems like you've got it all together, and in many respects you have. But Leos, especially when young, can be a bit like Apollo's son. You are so naturally confident and exude such optimism, it's unthinkable that anything can go wrong. It can take a few trials and errors for you to accept that even *you* are still learning and growing.

While you are accustomed to being the centre of attention, you never try to stop others from shining; in fact you love nothing more than bringing a little sunshine into the lives of others.

You appreciate that every individual is unique and always encourage others to be the best they can be, but at the same time it's also quite natural for you to feel a little bit superior. After all, you are a lion, the king

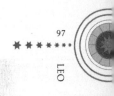

of the beasts and your ruling planet is the Sun, which is actually a star and not a 'lowly' planet.

Like the Sun, it's your role to give out light and warmth, which support life. All the planets revolve around the Sun so you possess a strong sense of self. There's an aura about you that can make you seem larger than life.

When the Sun is shining we feel good about life. We feel happy and positive and we're confident that everything will turn out for the best. Because the Sun is your ruling plant, you feel like this most of the time, even when storm clouds are gathering.

It's therefore quite natural that you should have a high opinion of yourself; however, you also need to be aware that you are but one of many stars in the universe. Our Sun is, in fact, just an average yellow star and there are countless other suns, some large and some small, and they're all at different stages of their life cycle.

Ultimately, while you are accustomed to being the centre of attention, you love nothing more than bringing a little sunshine into the lives of others.

We tend to think of the Sun as being fixed in the sky, but it's in orbit too, travelling around the centre of our Milky Way galaxy. It takes around 230 million years for the Sun to traverse our galaxy, taking all the planets, including us, along for the ride. The Sun is big. It constitutes some 99.9 per cent of the mass of our solar system, yet interestingly appears to be the same size as the Moon from our perspective on Earth, which is why astrologers consider the Moon and Sun as having equal significance.

The glyph for the Sun ☉ looks like an all-seeing eye, hence our Sun sign, be it Leo or any other sign, is the sign of which we are most consciously aware.

WHAT MAKES YOU TICK?

Leo children love showing off their many talents. They especially love performing, particularly on stage or in the sporting arena. You enjoy being in the limelight and love to have an audience. Having an audience helps you to see yourself, as you learn from other peoples' feedback. Just as the Moon and planets reflect the light of the Sun, when people respond to you, you learn to see yourself as others do.

Leos like to test their strength and love competing. Fire signs are accustomed to being first and so, in any competition, you expect to win, but you also have a great appreciation for individual effort and always give others a sporting chance.

You always give others a sporting chance.

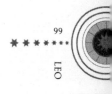

Optimistic and outgoing, you invariably look on the bright side. You know that to be successful in life, it's important to put your best foot forward and because you expect to win, you usually do.

Lions live in groups called 'prides' and Leos are indeed proud creatures. You take pride in both your achievements and in your appearance.

You like the best things in life and spare no expense. You enjoy gift giving just as much as spending money on yourself. Leos like to shop for clothes and jewellery and enjoy regular visits to the hairdresser. Male or female, Leos often have very beautiful hair. It might be straight or curly, but it's often thick and worn long, just like a lion's mane.

You like the best things in life and spare no expense.

People can learn a lot about you by observing the behaviour of cats. Like cats, you value your independence, but you also like to cuddle up close to those you love. Just like cats, you love to play, adore being pampered and groomed, and expect the best in life.

Now and then you might get into the occasional catfight as a way to test your strength. These contests often involve a feline of the opposite sex and are part of the courtship ritual, which is an important aspect of your life.

Lions live in groups called 'prides' and Leos are indeed proud creatures. You take pride in your both your achievements and in your appearance.

In life and in love you accept that you have to fight for what you want, and you enjoy the competition. Most of the time you come up trumps; in fact you're so accustomed to winning that it can be a shock to the system when you don't. There are times, however, when you are injured in battle and must return home to lick your wounds and heal.

It's a funny thing about Leos and their health, but there are two basic responses; either you totally ignore symptoms and soldier on regardless, or you dramatise the symptoms out of all proportion.

Leos possess abundant energy and strength—in fact your sign is one of the most robust and healthy.

Leos possess abundant energy and strength—in fact your sign is one of the most robust and healthy—but when you are under the weather it's almost as if you are not sure how to react.

The eminent Swiss psychologist, Carl Jung, was a Leo. Just as the sun illuminates, Jung's aim was to shed light on the unconscious. His whole life was spent investigating the unconscious, from which consciousness emerges and grows. He called this process 'individuation', the process of becoming oneself.

Maybe it's because you are so used to being strong that you think you're an invincible superhero. Or maybe it's because Virgo, the sign after Leo, is the sign of health, and as Virgo is your blind spot you have difficulty coming to terms with anything associated with health or healing.

Whatever the reason, facing pain, whether physical or emotional, is often difficult for Leos. Perhaps this is because deep down you are a sensitive kitten, or maybe you are so accustomed to being in the sunshine that when dark times come, you're not entirely sure what to do.

Your enthusiasm is completely natural and highly contagious.

A good proportion of Leos are genuinely uncomfortable around sick people and many have a real fear of doctors and hospitals—let's face it, hospital is a good place to avoid if we can—but like the lion with the thorn in its paw, when you are injured or sick, you should seek help. Very soon your energy and vitality will return to full strength for you are incredibly resilient.

Your sign is imbued with many talents and you thrive on praise and encouragement. Your enthusiasm is completely natural and highly contagious. You spread happiness and joy wherever you go and make the most of your opportunities.

Every sign of the zodiac contains positive and negative qualities and your sign is no exception. One of the negative traits of your sign is the tendency to be overly self-absorbed. It's just that the Sun is so big and radiant and dazzling, sometimes it can be difficult for you to see beyond yourself.

But at the same time you shine in leadership roles of all kinds. Many Leos are found running their own businesses, or in politics. Leadership comes naturally to you.

Leos are known for their generosity too. You appreciate quality and whether you are shopping for yourself, or for a loved one, money really is no object.

You enjoy lavish entertaining and have a real flair for presentation. Whatever the occasion—Christmas, birthdays, anniversaries, it really doesn't matter—you want to ensure everyone has a good time.

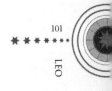

You like to organise parties and celebrate special occasions, arrange the menu and plan the whole effect, but when it comes to the finer points, you're more likely to call in the caterers and hire companies to manage the rest.

You much prefer to be the supervisor, so your vision stays intact, but handballing the details to someone else can be asking for trouble. Sure, delegating is sometimes necessary, and even desirable, but when you delegate, you're no longer fully in control, and this can be when problems can start, for you like to be in control of your own creative projects. You are the king, and others are your subjects, so it's natural you should want them to do your bidding—but at the same time you are also giving away your power.

You shine in leadership roles of all kinds.

The thing you need to learn is to stay true to your vision and also manage the finer points yourself. When you learn how, you begin to really grow in consciousness, which is, after all, one of your main aims in life.

Sometime around midlife you might begin to wonder how you can develop the skills to deal with the small stuff. It's simple really; all you have to do is listen to the advice and observe the behaviour of the Virgos you meet. As you get older, probably after you have children, or even grandchildren, you might learn how to focus your attention on one small thing at a time.

THE REALLY IMPORTANT THINGS IN YOUR LIFE

Love, children and art

Love is as vital to you as sunshine; you cannot live without it. You're a romantic and passionate creature and you wear your heart on your sleeve.

Having a committed relationship brings out the best in you. You are incredibly loyal; fidelity is a key ingredient in your relationship. You're affectionate and giving, but it's equally important that you feel appreciated and loved in return.

Courtship is something you take very seriously. You adore wining and dining, romantic candlelit dinners, impromptu weekend escapes, the giving and receiving of gifts—indeed, all expressions of love.

> *Love is as vital to you as sunshine; you cannot live without it.*

Next comes the proposal on bended knee; the dazzling engagement ring; the white dress with all the trimmings; the grand wedding reception, with all your family and friends in attendance. Every aspect of the ritual is important. Marriage brings out the best in you.

Most Leos are keen to be parents, and like lions and lionesses, strive to keep the family unit together.

Having been through the Cancerian experience, you appreciate the value of home and family, and you're keen to carry on the family tradition by having children of your own. Leos often view having children as the ultimate creative act.

> *Watching your children grow and seeing their conscious awareness develop is one of your greatest joys in life.*

As a parent you are proud of your children and their accomplishments and make every effort to encourage and support them. Some Leo parents can push their children too far and turn into the archetypal football father, or stage mother, but most know how important it is to allow their children the freedom to be individuals and to follow their own hearts.

Watching your children grow and seeing them develop is one of your greatest joys in life.

Of course, children don't come with an instruction book, but you don't mind, for you just do what comes naturally, and the same applies in all aspects of your life.

Leos often view having children as the ultimate creative act.

Many Leos are often naturally gifted in at least one, if not several, art forms and especially enjoy acting, performing and music. Of course, not all Leos are artistic, but even if you have no musical or artistic talents, you still love and appreciate all art forms and enjoy regular visits to galleries and the theatre.

Love, creativity and children are the three things that make your world go around. These are all different ways you can express your unique individuality, which for you is what life is all about.

You have many natural talents, and everything you do, you do wholeheartedly. In whichever way you choose to express yourself, above all you must be true to your heart.

SHARING YOUR KNOWLEDGE

How you get along with others

People you can teach:	Water signs—Cancer, Scorpio, Pisces
Compatible similar signs:	Fire signs—Aries, Leo, Sagittarius
Compatible complementary signs:	Air signs—Gemini, Libra, Aquarius
People you can learn from:	Earth signs—Taurus, Virgo, Capricorn

Relating to water signs (Cancer, Scorpio, Pisces)

Since the water element comes before the fire element, you understand the nature of water. It is the source of life so you feel you can count on water signs to support you. Water and fire are instinctive, right-brained elements, so you share a common understanding.

Water signs, however, are yin, while you are yang, which means you want them to be more outgoing and express themselves with as much confidence as you.

Cancerians, Scorpios and Pisceans can all benefit from your influence, though relationships with Scorpios will prove particularly challenging. Scorpios will never admit they need your help, but when they are feeling down, you can lead them out of their dark mood and into the light.

Water signs on the whole are reluctant to take action until they feel completely ready to do so. Most of the time you are patient with them, because you understand where they are coming from, but you still wish they were more like you. You can become frustrated by their seeming lack of initiative.

The combination of water and fire is a dynamic and sometimes volatile mix of elements, because water can put out fire and fire can make water boil.

Yet on the whole you appreciate these gentle souls for who they are, and are often unconsciously drawn to them, for they are the source of your inspiration.

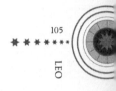

Relating to fire signs (Aries, Leo, Sagittarius)

Relationships with fire signs are fun, but you do need to be aware that too much fire can become destructive if it gets out of hand. What starts out as a warm, cosy campfire can escalate into a raging bushfire if you are not paying close attention.

What starts out as a warm, cosy campfire can escalate into a raging bushfire if you are not paying close attention.

Fire signs are naturally competitive, a tendency which is amplified when a few of you get together.

However, you are happy and at your best when there are fire signs in your life, for you appreciate their positive outlook.

Relating to air signs (Gemini, Libra, Aquarius)

Air helps fire to burn, so these people encourage you to be yourself. Like you, air signs are yang, sociable and outgoing.

Geminis, Librans and Aquarians are, however, usually left-brained, while you are mostly right-brained, which means there are enough differences between you to keep life interesting.

Air signs, while encouraging you to be yourself, can also help you manage details without actually taking over.

Geminis and Librans are an especially good match for you. Aquarius is your opposite sign and that means you often bring out the very best or very worst in one another, so this relationship requires a real mutual appreciation of your differences to stand the test of time.

Relating to earth signs (Taurus, Virgo, Capricorn)

It's the earth signs you have the most difficulty understanding. You have virtually nothing in common and hold contrasting views on every conceivable subject. You also have different values and ways of seeing the world. Yet in spite of, indeed because of, these fundamental differences, it's the earth signs who have the most to teach you.

You have to admit that when it comes to managing money and sorting out the nuts and bolts of your day-to-day responsibilities, you're really not that interested. The reason you are not interested is because you're actually not that good at it.

Though you have many talents, self-discipline is not one of them. You'd much rather spend money than save, and are more naturally inclined to focus on the big picture rather than the small stuff.

Although earth signs will drive you to distraction with their criticism, tendency to harp on about details, constant worrying about the future—and a thousand other irritating quirks—you really are only seeing the worst in them because you don't understand them. Actually, they want to teach you the life skills you lack.

WHAT YOU NEED TO LEARN
How to manage details

It's a funny thing, but have you ever noticed that the larger and more comprehensive your particular creative project is, the more and more details seem to be involved? It's Murphy's Law. Everything is connected, and that includes the macro and the micro.

Because you focus on the big stuff you avoid reading the fine print, hoping that some nice Virgo will come along to sort out the mess afterwards. And they often do, but by then it's too late; you are no longer in charge. Somehow, without any warning, they have taken over! Then you get all hot under the collar and start to growl and roar, which doesn't solve anything.

Let's look at this problem from another perspective. Let's say, for instance, you have found yourself in need of some money for an important business venture. Perhaps you need some expert advice, or a loan, so you decide to pop in to see the bank manager.

You are told to take a number and wait your turn and then when you finally get to speak to someone, they tell you to make an appointment. But you have important things to do! You should be served right away! Who do these people think they are?

This problem can arise at the doctors or at the supermarket, or any time you have to wait your turn.

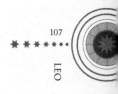

Virgos know better than anyone that we all make mistakes, and that means you.

These are some examples of how earth signs frustrate you. Virgo is the sign of service and service involves taking care of all those little things that need taking care of. There is a step by step process involved. Believe it or not, they're here to help you; in fact Virgos are probably the most organised and efficient sign of the zodiac. You just don't appreciate that details are important, and that they don't take care of themselves. Focusing on details is hard work; the kind of work you'd much rather avoid.

The nearest planet to the Sun is Mercury, Virgo's ruling planet. It's so small compared to the Sun and spins so fast around the Sun that you're completely oblivious to its presence, and it's the same with Virgos. You don't really see, nor appreciate, what they are trying to do.

Virgos know better than anyone that we all make mistakes, and that means you too. Sometimes you have trouble admitting it—you are, after all, the star of the show—so when those nitpicking Virgos hone in, so precisely, on exactly what is wrong, and point it out in no uncertain terms that you have actually made an error, well, you are apt to take it personally, for how can anyone be better than you?

Virgos and the other earth signs really do appreciate your talents, otherwise why would they spend their time tweaking and improving what you have created? Why would they run about trying to organise all those small things you can't be bothered attending to. All they want to do is to create order from chaos. They are not interested in pulling the rug out from under you. They're here to remind you that you are not really a superhero, but completely human and learning just like the rest of us.

TAKING THE NEXT STEP

You're so proud, it can be difficult for you to admit when you are wrong and that sometimes you need help. Whether you like it or not, there are people who are better at certain things than you.

Luckily, they have your best interests at heart. Virgos are the most helpful people in the whole zodiac, but you don't see it that way. Mostly they drive you crazy with their nitpicking, but they are actually trying to get you to realise those important details you have overlooked.

In the end it doesn't matter who's the boss; sometimes we learn the most valuable lessons from those we think are the least qualified to give advice.

Where would you be without them?

There is more to astrology than just the Sun sign. There are lots of planets and asteroids in our solar system and they are all located in one sign or another.

Mercury and Venus, for example, are never far away from the Sun, so it's quite possible that you might actually have some planets in Virgo yourself, many Leos do. Virgos can help you develop the talents you never knew you had.

They can also help you understand something about the other two earth signs. Taureans are fixed like you, which can make for a difficult relationship, yet they're also artistic and creative like Leos. Capricorns think they are the boss, but you know that you are really the one in charge, so this relationship can be tricky too—but Capricorns can show you that taking on responsibilities yourself can be empowering.

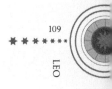

There are people in the world who are more skilled, more intelligent and more talented than you, and when you give credit where credit is due, you grow beyond your solar radiance, and your consciousness grows. After all, this is one of your chief aims in life.

In the end it doesn't matter who's the boss; sometimes we learn the most valuable lessons from those we think are the least qualified to give advice.

Though you might struggle to manage the small stuff, over time you can learn to appreciate the little things in life.

TIPS FOR LEO

♌ Now and then try attending to details yourself rather than delegating.
♌ Become a volunteer.
♌ Recognise that managing the small stuff once in a while can be empowering.

♌ Try blending creativity with detail, perhaps fine work like jewellery making.

♌ Once in a while do a jigsaw puzzle, it will help you to organise the small stuff.

♌ When you are in pain or unwell, visit a doctor or naturopath.

♌ Consider the advice of the earth signs you meet.

YOUR GIFT TO THE WORLD

How you can make a real difference

Your special gift to the world is your capacity for love. You inspire others and help them to shine. If there were only Leos living on Earth, the world would be an amazing place filled with love and boundless opportunities. Everyone would be successful, loved, happy and creatively fulfilled.

Though you might struggle to deal with the small stuff, your generosity and warmth win you admirers wherever you go.

FAMOUS PERSONALITIES WITH THE SUN IN LEO INCLUDE:

Neil Armstrong

Halle Berry

Napoleon Bonaparte

Bugs Bunny

Fidel Castro

Kim Cattrall

Bill Clinton

Robert De Niro

Roger Federer

Alfred Hitchcock

Stanley Kubrick

Mick Jagger

C.G. Jung

Lawrence of Arabia

Cecil B. DeMille

Madonna

Helen Mirren

Benito Mussolini

Barack Obama

Peter O'Toole

Robert Redford

J.K. Rowling

Arnold Schwarzenegger

George Bernard Shaw

VIRGO

24 AUGUST–23 SEPTEMBER

'We're all in this alone.'
Virgo, Lily Tomlin

YOUR LIFE MISSION

To perfect yourself and everything that you create and encounter. To be the best person you can be.

As a Virgo your focus is on developing your self-expression and skills to the highest standards you can reach. You have brilliant powers of discrimination and analysis. Your task is to use these gifts to be the best person you can be and to make improvements to anything that needs putting right.

Whether it's writing letters to the newspaper complaining about the latest toxic spill, voicing your concerns at the supermarket because they don't stock your favourite organic products, or venting your spleen to the council because there are not enough dog-poo bags at your local park, a million little things need your attention. No sooner do you fix one problem than another one crops up. Naturally, it's up to you to sort things out properly.

You're self-sufficient and resourceful and you want to do everything as quickly and efficiently as possible. That way there's no need to repeat anything, nor waste precious resources. You know life is short and you want to make every precious moment count. You have a talent for what my grandfather used to call 'uncommon sense'. Uncommon, because there isn't that much good sense around; it's a rare gift and you have a knack for using it wisely.

Your focus as a Virgo is to develop your self-expression and skills to the highest standards you can reach. Your task is to make improvements to anything that needs putting right.

To fulfil your life mission to be the best you can be, you naturally focus on essentials. For you, life is about priorities. You like to set your own goals, achieve them, and then move on to the next item on the list. But what often happens is that other people have the annoying habit of getting in the way and causing disruptions.

It's not that you dislike people, but they often frustrate you and interfere with your plans. You especially become annoyed if people start playing mind games.

Sometimes relationships can seem like an unnecessary distraction. You feel happier when you are just left alone to get on with things. But does this mean you are destined to be a hermit? How can you be true to yourself and also develop meaningful personal relationships?

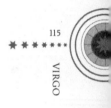

GIFTS FROM THE PAST

If you are born a Virgo it means you have inherited a lifetime of Leo wisdom. You know everything you need to know about yourself. Leo forged your identity and individuality, laying a foundation upon which you will now build. Now you want to be of service and to do all you can to attain excellence.

What you have already learned

- *To have a strong sense of self*
- *To be your own person*
- *That you are essentially a creative being*
- *To value your independence*
- *Clarity of vision*
- *To give of yourself generously*
- *Keen observation skills*
- *That overlooking details can cause problems*

ELEMENTS OF CHARACTER

Your special place in the zodiac

The sixth sign

Virgo is the sixth sign of the zodiac. The first half of the zodiac is about personal development, while the six signs that follow are more concerned with the wider world, with social issues, relationships and the community. Because Virgo is the last sign to focus on personal matters, and in order to fulfil your mission to be the best you can be, you feel compelled to act now. You know time is of the essence.

You have a sixth sense when it comes to spotting those annoying mistakes that everyone keeps making.

This is why it's so important for you to be organised and efficient, and why you have a sixth sense when it comes to spotting those annoying mistakes that everyone keeps making—that is, everyone except you and other Virgos.

Mutable earth

Virgo is a mutable sign, which means you are changeable and adaptable. All four mutable signs—Gemini, Virgo, Sagittarius and Pisces—are restless and flexible, but Virgo is the least so, because your mutability is balanced by the stability and grounded energy of the earth element.

You're probably not into collecting because possessions just create clutter and collect dust.

The earth element makes you practical and reliable, but of the three earth signs—Taurus, Virgo and Capricorn—your sign is the least concerned with money, status and material possessions. With the possible exception of books, you're probably not into collecting, because possessions just create clutter and collect dust.

You seem quiet, but there's a lot going on underneath the surface; you can occasionally erupt.

This unique mix of mutability and earthiness explains why people can misunderstand you. But it makes perfect sense to you because a mutable earth is a gradually evolving earth. You are also evolving. Like a smouldering volcano, or the pressure that builds up in the Earth's crust along its fault lines, you seem quiet, but there's a lot going on underneath the surface. You seldom get angry, but just like a volcano you can occasionally erupt.

Though you're a self-contained person, you soon learn there's nothing to be gained from bottling things up.

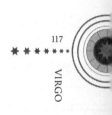

YOUR GODS AND MYTHS

Astrology fascinates many Virgos. You just love systems that explain how things work. You're naturally curious to understand more about yourself and the world around you.

People see your cool, calm and organised manner and assume you are aloof and cold. They are very much mistaken.

Virgos adore puzzles and mysteries, but at the same time you can be a bit of a puzzle yourself. There's some confusion about the true nature of Virgo, which stems from the idea that Virgos are pristine, pure and innocent, not to mention celibate and holy. These ideas mainly come from our Christian tradition, but astrology is far more ancient than Christianity.

Actually, it's wholeness, not holiness, that's important to you. But because of Christian and other influences, Virgos can have issues when dealing with sex and matters can be made worse by others' expectations. People see your cool, calm and organised manner and assume you are aloof and cold. They are very much mistaken. Actually, you are one of the most sensual creatures of the zodiac, but you are also an introvert and somewhat shy. Often you hide your sexuality from others, and sometimes even from yourself.

Ceres—Goddess of grain

Ceres/Demeter[1], was the goddess of crops and grain. She's usually pictured holding a stalk of wheat symbolising the harvest. Harvest time takes place when the Sun is in Virgo. It's a time of hard work, which is something you know all about. Most Virgos care deeply about animals and the environment. Ceres is the perfect symbol for your passionate interest in nature.

Mercury—Messenger of the gods

Mercury/Hermes[2] is your traditional ruler. Mercury teaches you to see beneath the surface of things. He was the only god who could journey to the Underworld and return unharmed, but he was best known as a trickster. He rules both Gemini and Virgo and gives to both signs a love of learning and language. But that's where any similarity ends. Geminis and Virgos are as different as dragonflies and onions.

Though both signs share Mercury as a ruling planet, Geminis and Virgos are as different as butterflies and onions.

Geminis will debate an issue purely for the fun of it, sometimes changing their point of view in mid-sentence. But you only argue the point when there is an important fact in dispute and when you know beyond a shadow of a doubt that you are right and the other person is wrong. Other people find it irritating, but 99 per cent of the time you will win a debate. The other 1 per cent you will credit because you know that you can always learn more.

Vesta—Virgin goddess of the hearth

Another celestial influence is Vesta/Hestia, who was the goddess of the hearth and keeper of the eternal flame. Vesta was the first-born of Saturn/ Cronus and the last to be regurgitated by her tyrant father after he swallowed his children. Vesta spent more time within her father than any of her sisters or brothers. This is why you are so self-contained, and also why you like to spend time alone.

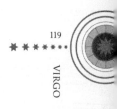

It's important to keep reminding yourself that virginity is not something to be taken literally. It's a symbol of your need for independance and self-sufficiency.

Vesta was the only goddess who never became involved in disputes or wars. Likewise, you're not really interested in political intrigues, or gossip.

Although she remained a virgin, Vesta had several suitors including Neptune/Poseidon, but she never had any intention of marrying. Many Virgos identify with Vesta and choose to remain single.

In Rome, Vesta was honoured within every home and public building where her eternal flame would burn.

The Vestal Virgins were the keepers of the sacred flame in Vesta's temple. The Romans believed that bad luck would befall their city if the eternal flame went out, so Vestal Virgins had an important job.

Young girls entered the temple before the age of ten and served for 30 years. After retirement, they were free to marry, but most chose to stay within the temple for the rest of their lives.

Vesta was very intent on retaining her independence. Her eternal flame represents your capacity for focus; in fact the Latin word for 'hearth' is focus.[3]

It's important to keep reminding yourself that virginity is not something to be taken literally. It's a symbol of your need for self-sufficiency. You don't need a relationship to feel fulfilled, for you are whole already. Yet, at some point you'll have fulfilled your duties and obligations and start to wonder what comes next. Later in life you might begin to realise you both need and want a relationship—fortunately, it's never too late.

WHAT YOUR PLANETS REVEAL ABOUT YOU

Ceres is the largest asteroid. When it was discovered on 1 January 1801, astronomers thought they had found a new planet. Recently, they considered giving Ceres planetary status again when the debate about Pluto's classification was raging.

In the myth of Pluto's abduction of Proserpina, Ceres and Pluto eventually came to an agreement to share Proserpina, so in a way it makes perfect sense that astronomers have decided that Ceres and Pluto should have equal status, as dwarf planets.

Perhaps now, as in the myth, Ceres will begin to return nourishment and fertility to our depleted Earth.

You have Mercury to thank for your unquenchable thirst for knowledge and lightning-quick mind.

Vesta is the second largest asteroid among the thousands orbiting between Mars and Jupiter. This small, volcanic world with its reflective surface shines just like the eternal flame and is the only asteroid that can be seen with the naked eye.

The entire asteroid belt can be linked to your sign because asteroids are small fragments of what may once have been a whole planet, or remnants from the origin of the solar system that never formed into a planet. Other asteroids like Hygeia, named after the goddess of healing, are also associated with Virgo.

NASA is planning a mission to Ceres and Vesta. The Dawn Mission is scheduled to visit these two small worlds, arriving at Vesta when the Sun is in Virgo, in September 2011.[4]

Mercury[5], your traditional ruling planet, is a small, hot world that orbits rapidly, very close to the Sun. You have Mercury to thank for your unquenchable thirst for knowledge and lightning-quick mind.

Mercury is never more than 28 degrees away from the Sun, which means it's always in either the same sign as the Sun or in the sign preceding or following it.

If Mercury was in Virgo when you were born, your Virgo qualities will be enhanced and strengthened. If Mercury was in Leo on the day you were born, you are a more outgoing, dynamic and creative kind of Virgo, such as Shania Twain, Cameron Diaz and Jimmy Connors.

If your Mercury is in Libra, you are a more diplomatic type of Virgo who is probably better at relationships than other Virgos. Richard Gere and Sophia Loren are examples.

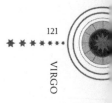

WHAT MAKES YOU TICK?

As a child you probably asked 'why' all the time, driving your parents mad with questions they had no hope of answering. Most likely you were content to play on your own, and you were probably a good student.

Before other children your age, you were probably thinking about your career prospects. One Virgo child I know wants to be an architect and enjoys drawing floor plans. Career options are many and varied because all Virgos are seriously dedicated to work and need the mental stimulation it provides.

Although you enjoy putting things in order, the idea that you are the neat freak of the zodiac is overstated. You have better things to do than to spend all your time cleaning.

When confronted by a problem, you always try to fix it yourself before asking for help, even if you have no idea about how to proceed. Over the course of a lifetime you are likely to develop a range of skills. Many Virgos are late bloomers, but eventually you might specialise in a niche area. You prefer to learn about a subject thoroughly, so you avoid making mistakes.

Queen Elizabeth I was a Virgo and was in many ways the literal embodiment of the symbolism of the virgin. She never married, nor did she have children. She also possessed the Virgo passion for learning. Elizabeth was highly respected as a scholar and spoke several languages. Many notable writers are born under your sign too; Agatha Christie, Stephen King, D.H. Lawrence and Leo Tolstoy to name a few.

You are an intelligent and highly conscious individual, capable of intense concentration. You are also rather particular and choosey. Virgos are selective about all kinds of details, including grammar, spelling, money matters, hygiene, diet, litter, health, work and relationships.

There's that word again—relationships. It's always in the back of your mind and the last thing you seem to get around to. Often it sits in the too-hard basket. You know it's there, of course, but it's down at the bottom of the pile. Meanwhile other things keep coming in that are more urgent and easier to deal with.

Then there's all that reading you have to catch up on. You enjoy self-help books, how-to manuals, biographies, history, magazines, journals and fiction. People will often find you browsing bookstores or at the library, and will be impressed by your extensive book collection. Naturally, your non-fiction titles will be arranged according to subject matter and the fiction sorted neatly according to author.

Many Virgos are late bloomers. You prefer to learn about a subject thoroughly, so you avoid making mistakes.

Although you enjoy putting things in order, the idea that you are the neat freak of the zodiac is probably overstated. You have better things to do than to spend all your time cleaning. 'Highly organised' is a better way to describe you.

Perhaps your sign is more likely to develop obsessive-compulsive disorders than other signs, but mostly you just accept that living is a messy business and arrange things so that they are easy to manage. Having a spotless home is less important to you than being able to locate things quickly when required.

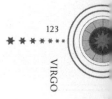

People get the impression you are interfering and pushy when all you really want to do is remedy imperfections.

Sometimes you can be overly fussy and critical. When you encounter any system that is inefficient, you immediately see how it can be done more effectively, with less waste, and will set about rectifying the problem. This can rub other people the wrong way, because they get the impression you are interfering and pushy when all you really want to do is remedy imperfections.

You are great at seeing flaws, but when *you* are criticised you tend to withdraw, feeling hurt and disillusioned. In your book, criticism is destructive—unless, of course, you are giving the critique. Eventually you will learn to focus on issues that really matter, and leave it to other Virgos to attend to the rest.

Although you are quite capable of adapting to change, sudden or unexpected change can cause you stress and make you run about trying to nail things down. One of your greatest strengths, however, is that you always keep a cool head in a crisis.

Whether in an emergency or simply dealing with day-to-day business, one day you will realise that you can't fix all the imperfections you encounter. In fact, you will probably become more relaxed and adaptable as you reach midlife, which is often when Virgos start to blossom.

> *One of your greatest strengths is that you always keep a cool head in a crisis.*

All Virgos hate waste. This includes resources such as money and energy, and especially time, which probably has something to do with Vesta, who spent so long entombed within her father, Saturn, the lord of time. As time is a precious commodity, rarely, if ever, are you running late.

A Virgo client of mine always arrives half an hour early for her appointments. She can't help herself. It's not just when she comes to see me; everywhere she goes she allows too much time. She was even thinking about getting some therapy because in her eyes this was a flaw that needed fixing. Then she realised that by arriving early she gets some time alone to herself, which she craves. Now she's happy to spend the extra half hour taking a short walk, meditating, planning her week or reading the newspaper.

> *As time is a precious commodity, rarely, if ever, are you running late.*

You can become stressed by the imperfections you encounter in other people and in the world generally, so it's important you have time alone on a regular basis. You are happy in your own company most of the time, but it's best not to overdo it, as this may not be so good for you psychologically.

Although you tend to avoid getting too close to people, you have a deep love for animals, and probably have a special pet. Whether dog, cat, fish or ferret, or something more exotic like a chameleon, you treasure all living things. But when and how will you form a truly meaningful relationship with a human companion?

> *It's important for you to have time alone on a regular basis.*

You're probably good with money too, but may dislike the idea of being in debt. If ever you do get around to a long-term relationship, it's probably a good idea to keep separate bank accounts, because that way you can maintain your financial independence. Naturally, your bank statements are reconciled and you will not hesitate to query any suspect transactions or bank fees that crop up.

Physically, Virgos have a youthful appearance, which is a by-product of your youthful attitude. Like your Capricorn cousins, you become more relaxed and easy-going as the years pass, and retain your youthfulness into midlife and beyond. You really are a great catch!

THE REALLY IMPORTANT THINGS IN YOUR LIFE

Work and health

Work comes first. You breathe it. You love it. It's your reason for getting up in the morning. You do many things well, but you're best suited to occupations in the health sector, animal welfare, the environment, domestic services, or professions involving communication, such as teaching, writing, publishing, the media or IT. You are highly efficient, enjoy variety and can tackle many tasks simultaneously. You are capable of working long hours, although you probably prefer to get things done as quickly as possible, as long as important details are not overlooked. You generate results because you approach tasks in a methodical way with a minimum of fuss; no other sign can match you for efficiency.

While you can be ambitious, this is not in the sense that others may interpret the word. You like to go at your own pace, which is faster than others think, and you prefer to challenge yourself against the clock, rather than to work against competitors. People sometimes think you are highly competitive, but in fact you are only driven by the desire to be the best you can be. You don't measure your achievements against others' standards, only according to your own internal benchmarks, which are the highest.

Work comes first. You breathe it. You love it. It's your reason for getting up in the morning.

So long as you're engaged in activities that provide mental stimulation and variety, you're quite content to work behind the scenes. In fact, being in the limelight can be stressful. You tend to assume that everything you do is being examined and criticised in the same way that you scrutinise every minute detail and notice every single mistake. Since you are already rectifying and perfecting, you don't relish the idea of being criticised. More often than not you are two steps ahead of the pack, having already considered other options and evaluated them as unworkable. So although you can be happy in a subsidiary role, you can also resent being told what to do, especially by those who are less capable than you. This is just about everyone, except other Virgos who tend not to be in positions of authority.

Though you love work, the workplace can be a source of stress, especially if you are not temperamentally suited to your occupation. Even though you do many things well, you soon learn this is not really the point. It's important that your work brings you fulfilment and a sense of personal reward. This is one of your most important lessons.

For the most part, you work best on your own. You support the adage 'too many cooks spoil the broth' and in fact you don't really understand the concept of teamwork.

In the early part of your working life you could find yourself in a routine job where you are not given the credit you deserve. This is partly because

you don't blow your own trumpet and partly because you find it difficult to stand up to others.

More often than not you are two steps ahead of the pack, having already considered other options and evaluated them as unworkable.

Because you are capable and intelligent, and like to be of service, you tend to take on too much work. You may even become a workaholic because of an unspoken need to show others how efficient or clever you are. But over time you will come to realise this is a waste of energy and time. You don't have to prove anything to anyone. But you do need to learn that perfection doesn't mean working yourself into the ground.

An unemployed Virgo is a very sad soul. But if you are out of work, either by choice or redundancy (very few Virgos are ever sacked), it's unlikely you will remain so for very long.

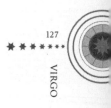

As you mature, any niggling health problems—real or imagined—tend to lessen and disappear.

If you are between jobs, you might try developing one of your many hobbies into a thriving business. Self-employment suits the Virgo temperament. Because you are highly organised and don't need much social contact, you can do things in far less time than it takes others. Working for yourself means you can go at your own pace and still take time out to smell the roses, walk the dog, do the crossword, or whatever revives your spirit and helps you focus. After a while, answering to employers who don't have any idea of what you are actually doing, or are capable of doing, can stick in the Virgo gut.

Work and health are interconnected. Nobody understands this better than you. At some point you may start to question the value of your job and lifestyle. This could begin with a build-up of stress and related health issues stemming from overwork. Sometimes you put yourself under a great deal of pressure that can even lead to hypochondria. But as you learn the importance of relaxation and laughter, niggling health problems—real or imagined—tend to lessen and disappear.

Self-employment suits the Virgo temperament.

Many Virgos take an active interest in healing and nutrition. Even though you are highly health conscious, you are still human. You are prone to conditions such as repetitive strain injury, recurring colds and sinus trouble, shoulder inflammation, digestive complaints, constipation, allergic reactions and intestinal disorders.

While you are aware of the need to eat well and to exercise regularly, try not to become hyper-focused on diet and health or take the idea of physical perfection too far. Virgos are prone to worry, so relaxation techniques such as yoga, Tai Chi or meditation can be particularly soothing and healing. Activities such as bushwalking, racquet sports or dance can be highly beneficial too. Like most other things in life, you prefer to exercise alone.

SHARING YOUR KNOWLEDGE

How you get along with others

People you can teach:	Fire signs—Aries, Leo, Sagittarius
Compatible similar signs:	Earth signs—Taurus, Virgo, Capricorn
Compatible complementary signs:	Water signs—Cancer, Scorpio, Pisces
People you can learn from:	Air signs—Gemini, Libra, Aquarius

Relating to fire signs (Aries, Leo, Sagittarius)

Once you master a skill, learn new information, figure out the best way to deal with a problem, or discover a useful insight, you are keen to help those who are still in the dark. Generally this assistance is provided to the fire signs, for they are the people who lack practical skills and the capacity to organise details.

Because you have an intrinsic understanding of the inner workings and motivations of fire signs and are sympathetic to their needs, you will often go out of your way to assist these people. You like to offer practical help whether or not you are asked. The only problem is that fiery people are more interested in spontaneous, creative expression and will strongly resist being organised in this way. Fire signs often feel smothered or restricted by your attempts to put their lives in order.

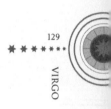

Fire/Earth relationships tend to be challenging, but fire signs are often the people you are most attracted to.

Even so, you will keep trying to rectify their problems, thinking you are being helpful—and you are. Part of you secretly hopes they will get their act together so you can move on. Fire/Earth relationships tend to be challenging, but fire signs are often the people you are most attracted to.

Relating to earth signs (Taurus, Virgo, Capricorn)

Many of your good friends are probably earth signs. They are your astrological brothers and sisters. You see eye to eye with these people and share a feeling of affinity. Even so, sometimes these relationships can become dull and predictable, especially those with other Virgos. You probably get along better with Capricorns than with Taureans, as some Taureans can be a little too stubborn and materialistic for your liking.

Despite this, you all have a great deal in common and you will probably develop long-standing friendships with Virgos, Taureans and Capricorns; however, there is little in the way of challenge or stimulation to be found in these relationships.

Relating to water signs (Cancer, Scorpio, Pisces)

Potentially, these relationships are the most harmonious and comfortable relationships you will encounter. All the water signs can show you how to get in touch with your emotions. When you are around these people, you feel as if you have permission to relax and express your feelings. Cancerians and Scorpios are especially compatible. Pisces is your opposite sign. Because opposites attract, Virgos are often fascinated by Pisceans, and they by you. Many people have at least one significant relationship with their opposite sign.

When you are around water signs, you feel as if you have permission to relax and express your feelings.

On the one hand, Pisceans can transport you to a magical place of dreams, filled with romance, beauty and unconditional love; on the other hand, they can drive you crazy because they are so disorganised and impossible to pin down.

Relating to air signs (Gemini, Libra, Aquarius)

Air signs will push your buttons, annoy you, pester you, and irritate you in a thousand different ways, but you can learn a lot from them if you pay attention.

If you are honest with yourself you'll admit that when it comes to relationships, you are not really so clever.

While you are highly self-aware and have numerous talents and abilities, if you are honest with yourself you'll admit that when it comes to relationships, you are not really so clever. Conflicts with the airy people in your life will teach you about other people and yourself. Relationships might seem like hard work, but help is at hand.

WHAT YOU NEED TO LEARN

Relationships

Let's face it, people can be incredibly annoying. You would rather be alone than put up with people who don't measure up to your high standards.

Relationships are your number one source of stress, and because they can be painful, you tend to avoid them, but you can take this self-sufficiency thing too far.

The more you withdraw, and the less you interact with others, the more your tolerance and social skills diminish. You might as well join a convent or a monastery. But hang on a minute; is that what you really want?

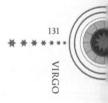

Relationships are your number one source of stress, and because they can be painful, you tend to avoid them, but you can take this self-sufficiency thing too far.

You have so much to offer. You need love and affection and, yes, a relationship, just like everyone else. At some point you will reach the bottom of your in-tray. You will have attended to everything on your to-do list. In the process, you have been preparing yourself for this next step. You *are* the best you can be. But when you get to that point and feel ready, just how do you go about finding that perfect relationship?

Because of your natural shyness, it is difficult for you to approach people. You often agonise over the best way to start a conversation. You're unsure just how to establish a connection, so what happens is that you tend to analyse relationships rather than letting them happen naturally.

TAKING THE NEXT STEP

What you need to know is that you can learn all about relationships from Geminis, Librans and Aquarians. These people can show you how to interact with others. Just as you want to help the fire signs become more organised, the air signs want to help you learn about people.

You may not realise it, but you have more in common with the air signs than you think. Just like you, they prefer to maintain their independence when they're involved in a relationship. But what they have, and you don't, is the ability to interact with ease in social situations, though you think these people are just so annoying you couldn't possibly learn anything from them.

Although you share Mercury as a ruling planet with Gemini, the Gemini/Virgo relationship is often fraught with problems. For starters, Geminis never shut up. They keep interrupting you every five seconds and think they know more than you, which of course they don't! But these pesky tricksters can teach you the art of conversation, especially small talk.

Aquarians also drive you wild because they create chaos everywhere they go, but they can show you how to connect with like-minded people, even groups of people. They have a social conscience, which you admire, and you share their interest in improving the future.

Sometimes you can be resistant to new ideas, information and technology. Air signs can teach you about these airy subjects too.

You think you have all the answers and anything you don't already know you would rather work out yourself.

Because they want you to evolve, they often tell you how to go about things, and that rubs you the wrong way. You think you have all the answers and anything you don't already know you would rather work out for yourself.

Virgo along with Gemini (twins) and Aquarius (water bearer) are the only three signs with human symbols. You all possess sharp minds that need exercising regularly. Yet this highly developed consciousness makes it difficult for you to get in touch with the physical aspects of your animal natures and emotions. You are more comfortable in your head than in your heart. But it is by opening your heart that you will find the love that you are seeking. Through your air sign friends you will learn how to connect with people, which is the first step.

Libra shares your love of order and desire for perfection, for they have already experienced what it's like to be a Virgo. But Librans know about people and relationships, which is your blind spot. You don't understand where they are coming from, or what makes them tick. On the one hand they seem to be entrepreneurial, have leadership qualities and the ability to socialise and network, but on the other, they seem to need others to motivate them and to be incredibly indecisive. Are they leaders or followers? It's just not clear whether they're more interested in 'what they know' or 'who they know'; maybe they're only interested in making a good impression? It's all very confusing to your sense of order and commonsense.

Air signs can teach you how to form closer relationships. These are the 'people' people of the zodiac. They value social interaction and teamwork, which is as foreign to you as suddenly finding yourself living on Venus, where the days are longer than the years. Venus looks so pretty from planet Earth, so shiny and radiant, but get too close and one could suffocate, be crushed to death, or be burned by the atmosphere of sulphuric acid! It seems much safer to keep your distance.

If you're honest with yourself, you'll admit that you lack skills in the area of teamwork and relationships and should allow the air signs to teach you about diplomacy, the value of networking and how to connect with others socially.

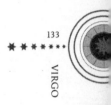

> *Being open to learning these skills from air signs doesn't mean you will suddenly turn into one.*

Don't worry, being open to learning these skills from air signs doesn't mean you will suddenly turn into one. To some extent, in order to maintain your inner focus, you will resist their help because like Virgo Greta Garbo, you want to be alone.

TIPS FOR VIRGO

♍ Try not to worry too much.

♍ Strike a balance between time spent alone and time with others.

♍ Every so often go out and meet new people, even if you don't feel like it.

♍ Remind yourself that you are beautiful and lovable on a regular basis.

♍ Give yourself a beauty treatment once in a while, or have a massage.

♍ When you don't know how to do something, ask for help.

♍ Consider the advice of the air signs you meet.

YOUR GIFT TO THE WORLD

How you can make a real difference

Your special gift to the world is your ability to create order from chaos. No matter the problem, you instinctively know the best way to tackle it. The world would be a much more peaceful, environmentally friendly and well-ordered place if only Virgos lived here. Everyone would be healthier, happier and more fulfilled.

While you probably do need to learn more about relationships, your real gift to the world is to set a personal example to others. Although you may not know it, by following your mission to be the best you can be, you are a source of inspiration and can make a real difference. Remind yourself of this often.

FAMOUS PERSONALITIES WITH THE SUN IN VIRGO INCLUDE:

Lauren Bacall
Anne Bancroft
Ingrid Bergman
Sir Donald Bradman
Agatha Christie
Sean Connery
Queen Elizabeth I
Greta Garbo
Richard Gere
Liz Greene
Chrissie Hynde
Samuel Johnson

Sister Kenny
Stephen King
D.H. Lawrence
Sophia Loren
Bill Murray
Keanu Reeves
Kevin Rudd
Peter Sellers
Victor Meldrew
Mother Theresa
Leo Tolstoy
H.G. Wells

LIBRA

24 SEPTEMBER–23 OCTOBER

'All's fair in love and war.'
LIBRA, FRANCIS EDWARDS SMEDLEY

YOUR LIFE MISSION

To establish harmonious relationships with others so you can spread justice, fairness and equality in a spirit of cooperation.

As a Libran your main interest is in other people and relationships. Life is not just about you anymore. There's a big wide world full of people and you want to get to know them. Having passed from Virgo into Libra, you are no longer working on personal development, you are much more focused on what makes others tick. Individual goals are of secondary importance.

You have fantastic people skills. Diplomacy and networking talents are among your greatest assets. It truly matters to you to be fair and just in all your dealings. Your task is to create a level playing field everywhere you go and to forge connections between people.

If you're truthful with yourself, you'll admit that ignoring problems doesn't make them go away.

You're a true idealist. 'Peace, harmony and justice' is your motto and you want people to cooperate with each other and share everything equally.

Whether it's personal relationships, business contacts or in family relations, you love it when everyone gets along with one another. But what often happens is that ugly emotions have the habit of simmering to the surface. Just as you are getting to know someone, nasty traits like jealousy, greed, selfishness or cruelty rear their ugly heads and make you duck for cover. You can't bear the dark side of human nature so you run a mile whenever a Medusa or Cyclops shows up, and don't they always?

*Whether it's jealousy, greed, selfishness or cruelty, you
can't bear the dark side of human nature.*

You prefer it when everyone smiles politely at each other. Your need for harmony is so vital to your sense of wellbeing, you seek it at any price, even if it isn't completely sincere.

But if you're truthful with yourself, you'll admit that ignoring problems doesn't make them go away. Conflict happens and emotions exist and just like everyone else, you also have feelings and even a dark side. Pretending everything is fine, when it isn't, doesn't solve anything.

So how can you take relationships to a deeper level of intimacy so that real connections can be established, without experiencing all the ugliness and pain? Is it possible to avoid all the suffering and unpleasantness in the world? And if you do manage to avoid it, are you really being truthful? How can you connect more deeply with people and your own feelings, while still maintaining your equilibrium?

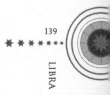

GIFTS FROM THE PAST

If you're a Libran, Virgo taught you to be a perfectionist. You're an idealist because you have already established exceptional standards of personal behaviour. But Virgos are not especially interested in what other people do; this is where you come in. It's your task to focus on the world around you, in particular its people, and to encourage high ideals and standards in others.

What you have already learned

- *To recognise what is perfect and what is not*
- *The importance of health and hygiene*
- *Excellent communication skills*
- *High standards of personal behaviour*

- *All about hard work*
- *That each individual can make a real difference*
- *That you don't want to be alone*

ELEMENTS OF CHARACTER

Your special place in the zodiac

The seventh sign

Libra is the seventh sign of the zodiac. The first half of the zodiac is interested in personal development, while the six signs that follow are more aware of society as a whole, relationships and the wider community. Your sign is the first in the zodiac to focus beyond your own needs, so whenever a discussion seems to be too one-sided, you always point out there's another way to view things. Being born under the seventh sign is another reason why you're interested in equality and balance, for Libra is the midpoint of the zodiac.

Cardinal air

Libra is a cardinal sign, which means you are the sort of person who takes the initiative. All four cardinal signs—Aries, Cancer, Libra and Capricorn—have excellent leadership skills, but because Libra is also concerned with people and relationships, you lead by joining forces with others. You aren't interested in leading on your own. It's important other people see the merits of your plans and adopt your causes.

The Sun moves into Libra at the autumn equinox, when day and night are of equal length, which is another reason why equality appeals to you.

This special mix of cardinality and air tells us a lot about you. You're a real people person; you're great at socialising and communicating. You really

SECRETS OF THE ZODIAC

enjoy interacting with your fellow humans. Air is the only element that has no animal symbolism, it's a human element, so you're highly civilised.

You're a rational and highly intellectual person, who has an excellent mind, and you're capable of seeing all sides of a problem. The Sun moves into Libra at the autumn equinox, when day and night are of equal length, which is another reason why equality appeals to you. You live your life according to the principle of fair play.

YOUR GODS AND MYTHS

Librans can be difficult to understand. Maybe you even have trouble understanding yourself. You can be full of contradictions. For one thing, your sign is a masculine sign, but ruled by Venus, a feminine planet.

You can be driven to achieve, but you're also eager to please. Sometimes you can be incredibly forceful, yet you can also be graceful and charming. You could become a radical activist, yet you are peace-loving and don't like to rock the boat.

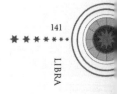

Athena—Goddess of wisdom

Minerva/Athena, the beloved daughter of Jupiter/Zeus, is a goddess with whom Librans often identify. Clever and impartial, goddess of wisdom and the arts, her symbol is the wise owl.

Athena is a cultured goddess, an intellectual who was in every respect the equal of men. She involved herself in politics and in war and other manly activities. To the Greeks she was, and is, the protector of the city of Athens.

You're a rational and highly intellectual person, who has an excellent mind, and you are capable of seeing all sides of a problem.

Libran women who identify with Athena can be very driven and career-minded; like Margaret Thatcher for example. But although she was tough-minded and had strong opinions, the Iron Lady was always softly spoken and impeccably groomed.

Venus—Goddess of love

Venus/Aphrodite[1] was the goddess of love and beauty. Aphrodite has two distinct faces. In some cultures Aphrodite was worshipped as the goddess of war and she often caused conflict. Eros and Aphrodite often worked together, making gods, heroes and mortals fall in love.

One story tells how Aphrodite was challenged by the beauty of a mortal named Psyche (which means Soul) whose beauty rivalled that of the love goddess herself. Like the queen in the fairytale of Snow White, Aphrodite was a jealous goddess with a dark side. When she heard there was another in the land who was more beautiful than she, she was so envious of poor innocent Psyche that she sent Eros to shoot an arrow at her and make her fall in love with a creature called Death. However, as luck would have it, Eros accidentally pricked himself with his own arrow and so he fell in love with Psyche.

*You **can** live happily ever after, but you can't experience equality, intimacy or a soul union if you avoid the pain of truly connecting.*

Although Eros was a god and Psyche a mortal, Eros told Psyche they could stay together in paradise, so long as Psyche never looked at him, nor asked him any questions. Naturally she agreed, but eventually curiosity got the better of her and when she looked at Eros she instantly fell in love with her husband, so Eros flew back to Aphrodite.

Aphrodite set Psyche four tasks as punishment for having dared to consider herself worthy of Eros. With a little help Psyche managed to complete the tasks, and was made immortal so she and Eros could stay together. They lived happily ever after with Aphrodite's blessing, and had a daughter they named Pleasure.

Psyche represents the innocent young beauty of youth, and Aphrodite the mature woman who has become a love goddess. Inside many a Libran, there's an innocent Psyche who is looking for love but is also in the process of becoming an Aphrodite.

This story tells us a lot about you and your relationships. So long as you remain innocent, everything seems like paradise.

When you really look at your partner, it can be painful, but you can only find true love and equality in your relationships when you see others for who they really are.

You *can* live happily ever after, but you can't experience equality, intimacy or a soul union if you avoid the pain of truly connecting. 'Psyche' means soul, and isn't that what you really want, a soul union?

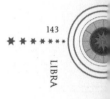

Themis—Goddess of justice

Themis is another goddess linked with Libra. She was the goddess of divine law and order. Themis is often depicted wearing a blindfold, holding the scales of justice and a sword. She governs the laws of civilised society.

When you are trying to decide where the truth lies, remember that appearances can be misleading.

Themis instructed humanity in justice, morality, etiquette, hospitality and social conduct; these are issues that concern you.

Your internal scales are always weighing and balancing, so making decisions can be an arduous process. Try to keep in mind that you hold a sword as well as scales. This can help you in the decision-making process. When you are trying to figure out where the truth lies, remember that appearances can be misleading. Themis wears a blindfold. This symbolises your need to be impartial. It also means that sometimes you need to look more deeply within yourself and beneath the surface of things to uncover the truth.

Libran men are often artistic and in touch with their feminine side. This happens when Libran men identify with Venus. Libran women, on the other hand, may identify with Athena, which makes them more competitive. These Libran women see themselves as the equal of men in every respect.

In some way all Librans need to find a middle ground in some essential part of their lives. This is why you have both a masculine and feminine side to your personality. You're always trying to balance yin and yang.

WHAT YOUR PLANETS REVEAL ABOUT YOU

Venus[2] is your ruling planet. Known as the Earth's twin, Venus and Earth are of similar size, but that's where the similarity ends.

Though you don't like to admit it, everything and everyone is a mixture of good and bad, and that includes you.

Venus is the most perfect sphere of all the planets in the solar system, and from a distance Venus is shiny and beautiful. The morning and evening star, Venus is the most dazzling jewel in the night sky.

But Venus is actually covered with dense toxic clouds of sulphuric acid. The atmospheric pressure would crush you the instant you arrived there, that is if you hadn't already spontaneously combusted from the intense heat. Venus is the hottest place in the solar system. It's fairly close to how we imagine hell.

Venus is never more than 48 degrees away from the sun. This means if you are a Libran, Venus will be in one of five signs: Leo, Virgo, Libra, Scorpio or Sagittarius. Your Venus sign modifies the type of Libran you are and reveals more about your temperament and personality.

As Venus is your ruling planet, you want to keep these dark energies at bay. You know if you get too close, these destructive forces can overwhelm you. Though you don't like to admit it, everything and everyone is a mixture of good and bad, and that includes you. The problem is that if you ignore the bad stuff, it will only intensify.

WHAT MAKES YOU TICK?

When you were a child you probably took on the job of peacemaker in the family. Maybe you are a middle child and this role came naturally to you. Most likely you were eager to please and keen to fit in with your peer group. You were probably a well-groomed, tidy child who enjoyed playing dress-up, had lots of friends, and minded your manners.

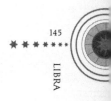

Events during puberty often play a significant role in shaping the Libran personality.

Events during puberty often play a significant role in shaping the Libran personality. Those first kisses and romantic stirrings open up the wonderful world of personal relationships, but they can also bring emotional pain to your life for the first time.

These early emotional scars can make it difficult for you to express your deeper feelings. For although you really want and need a relationship, all your positive emotions can become locked away with the more painful ones, and that makes it difficult for you to really connect with others.

You're popular, friendly, gracious and charming. People admire your good taste and pleasant smile and you go out of your way to make people feel good about themselves.

As a Libran, it's mandatory to share your life with another person. In fact it's pretty rare to meet a single Libran. Most marry young and a fair number marry several times. You have many admirers and you really don't like being alone. Your best qualities really shine when you are involved in a permanent relationship.

You like to know what people are doing and wearing, where the latest trendy café is—and you enjoy a good gossip too.

In an ideal world you'd love nothing more than to share everything equally, especially with your partner, but unfortunately we don't live in an ideal world. Problems can crop up, especially if there's an imbalance between give and take. Because it's so important for you to have a partner in your life, you really go out of your way to maintain harmony. When conflict happens, you are great at working out a compromise, but sometimes you pretend everything is fine when the reality is quite different.

The problem is you really don't want to acknowledge there's a dark side. It's too painful. But it's important to realise that emotions, when suppressed, can turn ugly. If you were more in touch with your feelings, and expressed them more often, your connection with others would deepen. As you mature, you'll start to realise that a perfect relationship doesn't mean never experiencing any conflict or having differences. Sometimes you have to agree to disagree.

Most Librans marry young and a fair number marry several times.

You truly respect other people and their views. No doubt you have lots of friends and acquaintances and you enjoy introducing your friends to each other and even playing matchmaker from time to time. You love spending time with people from all walks of life. You love to know what people are doing and wearing, where the latest trendy café is—and you enjoy a good gossip too. You generally give people the benefit of the doubt, though you simply can't abide anyone who is cruel, selfish or vindictive.

One reason why you like to mix with a variety of people is that it helps you figure out exactly where you fit in.

No other sign of the zodiac is as adept as you at networking. If someone wants to know the right person for the job, you will know who that is or you will easily be able to find out.

Because people really matter to you, when confronted by a problem, you like to ask other people what they did in similar situations because this information guides you in your own decision-making. You're intelligent and have superb powers of reasoning.

Likewise, you have no hesitation asking people for help when you need it, and you are first in line to provide others with assistance.

Although you want to live in a utopian world of peace and harmony, you also realise that if there never were any conflicts in life, you wouldn't have anything to do.

Like the preceding sign Virgo, you can be rather particular. You're meticulous and like the best of everything. Naturally, your home is beautifully decorated, clean and tidy. You love being surrounded by the finest quality. You're stylish and elegant and exude good taste.

Because you can become stressed by the injustice and ugliness in the world, it's important that you live in tranquil surroundings.

As far as work goes, you're suited to a career in politics, law, social services or law enforcement. You could also achieve success in the beauty industry, or in any artistic field, including interior or graphic design. Customer service and public relations are also good choices as working with people brings out the best in you. You know that many hands make light work and thrive on being part of a team. You might also consider working in a partnership arrangement, perhaps with your true love by your side.

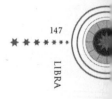

Political and spiritual leader and Libran Mahatma Ghandi adopted a policy of non-violent civil disobedience and non-cooperation in his fight for India's independence. Libran John Lennon was true to the ideals of peace and love. With songs like *Give Peace a Chance*, *War is Over* and *Imagine* Lennon communicated the Libran message of justice, equality, peace and harmony through his music and by peaceful protest; while Libran musician and political activist Bob Geldof is best known for organising Live Aid.

Many Librans are committed to working for an important cause.

Whether taking on the job of union delegate so that your colleagues are treated fairly, raising funds for a peace mission, or campaigning for animal rights, wherever you see an injustice you always step in. Whatever the problem, you know that equality and harmony can be restored if only people would make an effort. It's your role to encourage others to get involved.

Wherever you see an injustice you always step in.

Making time to get away from the pressure and rat race now and then restores your equilibrium and sense of perspective. When you do get away, you love nothing more than a weekend at a five-star resort where you can indulge your senses. Camping and backpacking are not really your style. Most Librans aren't keen on roughing it. You'll take a continental breakfast over a burnt offering of campfire toast any day.

Physically, Librans are often very beautiful, which is a gift from your ruling planet Venus. You enjoy spending time and money on your appearance and are always well presented. Sometimes you can be too focused on appearances. It's great to look nice, say the right thing and please others, but as you get older you will begin to see that appearances are not as important as you once thought they were and that you need to pay more attention to what is going on underneath the surface.

Psychologically speaking, if you always run away from your feelings, or fail to acknowledge them, this can lead to a build-up of toxins from stress. Not expressing anger, for example, can make you feel 'pissed off' and that can bring on psychosomatic health issues, such as kidney and bladder problems, including urinary tract infections. The skin is another vulnerable area for Librans.

Most Librans, however, enjoy excellent health. This is chiefly because you have inherited the Virgo wisdom of healing and nutrition. You understand the importance of a healthy diet and regular exercise, though sometimes you can overindulge in sweets and alcohol (so that's something you might need to watch).

Your internal scales are forever trying to find a happy balance, so you know that moderation in all things is the way to go. Even though you can be occasionally indulgent, you usually don't allow yourself the luxury of wasting too much time lazing about. There is important work to be done.

Working with people brings out the best in you.

Although you want to live in a utopian world of peace and harmony, as you mature you will begin to realise that if no conflict existed, you wouldn't have anything to do. You wouldn't be able to negotiate settlements, mediate, or fight for justice. And this insight will help you manage life's ups and downs.

In your attempts to be fair and just in your dealings, you can sometimes be incredibly indecisive. But as you mature you will start to peek beneath the surface of things to where your inner passions are stirring. As you grow older you'll also develop more insight into the hidden motives of other people and this will help you decide exactly where the truth lies.

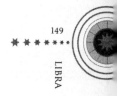

THE REALLY IMPORTANT THINGS IN YOUR LIFE

Relationships, justice and fairness

You know that love makes the world go around. You're a true romantic who'll do anything for love. You thrive in a beautiful atmosphere of peace and tranquillity where you and your partner can live happily ever after in paradise. This fairytale existence might seem like an impossible dream to other more practical signs of the zodiac, but you are forever searching for the ideal.

Even though you are totally committed to your current love interest, you're always on the lookout, just in case. All Librans love to flirt.

Being involved in a steady relationship means you are free to follow your ideals of justice and truth and even take on a leadership role. You can achieve just about anything, so long as you have support from others, particularly from your partner. If you're not involved in a relationship, which is hardly ever, you can feel rudderless and lost, not knowing which way to turn. Once your personal life is on track, you can get on with making the world a better place.

You know that love makes the world go around. You're a true romantic.

You care about those less fortunate. Social justice is high on your list of priorities. Because fair play is so important to you, when you feel unjustly dealt with, or more especially when you see that others have encountered injustice, you will not hesitate to take matters in hand. You're even capable of bending the law to your own sense of justice, if need be.

For a long time a Libran client of mine led a community campaign concerning a major pollution problem. He devoted hours and hours every week, for years, trying to get government action. It almost became a full-time job. He met with politicians, business leaders and government officials and liaised with the media. He organised community rallies and patiently listened to his neighbours' complaints. Over time he became more and more frustrated by the lack of action of the authorities.

He confided to me that he was considering taking some drastic action, actually breaking the law to make his point, but commonsense prevailed. He soon realised how much time and effort he had been putting in, and how unbalanced life had become. Not long after giving up the fight his enthusiasm and energy returned and he became involved in leading another community campaign.

You can achieve just about anything, so long as you have support from others, particularly your partner.

It's always the principles of justice that are important to you, not the literal letter of the law. If the law is unjust, you have no hesitation in lobbying for change, and if that doesn't work you'll consider taking the law into your own hands to make your point—but only if it becomes absolutely necessary, and no one gets hurt in the process. Like Libran Mahatma Ghandi, you always adhere to the principles of justice, fairness, equality and, above all, peace.

SHARING YOUR KNOWLEDGE

How you get along with others

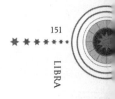

People you can teach:	Earth signs—Taurus, Virgo, Capricorn
Compatible similar signs:	Air signs—Gemini, Libra, Aquarius
Compatible complementary signs:	Fire signs—Aries, Leo, Sagittarius
People you can learn from:	Water signs—Cancer, Scorpio, Pisces

Relating to earth signs (Taurus, Virgo, Capricorn)

It's natural you should want to share your knowledge with others. As a rule you are keen to educate the earth signs because you can see how they have a hard time keeping up with the latest trends and lack your social graces.

Because you find it easy to communicate with earth signs and respect their logical minds, you go out of your way to help them. They won't ask for your assistance, but you are happy to give it anyway. Earthy people are more interested in doing things their own way and will resist being told anything different. Earth signs often feel stressed by your efforts to get them to be more sociable and outgoing.

Even though they can test your patience, you keep trying to help them. Earth/Air relationships can be challenging, but earth signs are the people you are most attracted to. You can relate to them intellectually, but these relationships usually stay on a head level and seldom deepen into emotional attachments.

Relating to air signs (Gemini, Libra, Aquarius)

You probably have lots of air sign friends and acquaintances. You love to chat and catch up for coffee and a gossip.

It goes without saying that air signs have a lot in common, but when two Librans get together it can be nearly impossible to decide who leads and who follows, let alone which way to go. Do you remember the cute little gophers Mac and Tosh from the Warner Brothers cartoons of the 60s? They were full of compliments for one another, always graceful and charming. Each of them always wanted the other one to go first. They could never make up their minds. Eventually they would decide to do everything together.

Relating to fire signs (Aries, Leo, Sagittarius)

Potentially, relationships with fire signs are the most fantastic relationships of your life. Fire signs encourage you to be more passionate and they're fun to be around. When you're with them, you're more dynamic. Leos and Sagittarians are especially compatible.

Aries is your opposite sign. Because opposites attract, you find Aries people quite interesting. They inspire you and spur you to action, but they also drive you mad because they're so impulsive. They never stop for a second to weigh up alternatives. They just jump straight in, which in your eyes is childish and irresponsible.

Relating to water signs (Cancer, Scorpio, Pisces)

Water signs frustrate you, confuse you and bring conflict into your life, but you can learn a lot from them if you are willing to open your heart.

While you are highly diplomatic, just and fair, if you are honest with yourself you'll admit that when it comes to emotions and feelings, you do have issues. Water signs want to teach you about feelings, which is dark and scary territory for you, but help is at hand.

WHAT YOU NEED TO LEARN

To feel passion

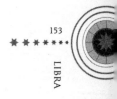

Be honest. Emotions terrify you. You only want to see the beauty in the world. Your life can be like a perpetual cocktail party. You love it when everyone smells nice, dresses for the occasion and discusses the latest movie or celebrity gossip, or even important issues like how to bring about world peace. But it's all on a head level. It's all surface gloss.

At some point you will realise that you can't avoid feelings and emotions by pretending they don't exist.

What are you feeling? What is really going on underneath? What are you really passionate about? The trouble is that dealing with emotions unbalances you. Up, then down, then up, then down again. Emotional rollercoasters make you feel sick!

Emotions are your number one source of stress, and because feelings can be painful, you want to avoid them. But the more you try to avoid unpleasantness, the more likely you are to encounter it. As much as you would like to, you simply can't have light without dark.

The trouble is that dealing with emotions unbalances
you. Up, then down, then up, then down again.
Emotional rollercoasters make you feel sick!

But even when you feel ready to peek into the world of feeling, just how do you go about it?

TAKING THE NEXT STEP

What you need to know is that you can learn all about emotions from Cancer, Scorpio and Pisces. These people are keen to show you how to get in touch with your passions and feelings. Just as you want to help the earth signs to be more social and outgoing, water signs want to help you learn about the deeper aspects of the human heart.

Air and water are the two most incompatible elements, so it's not easy for you to understand them. But what they have and you don't is an intrinsic sensitivity and ability to sympathise, not just intellectually but from the heart. You think these people are just so irrational; how can you possibly learn anything from them?

It's true they are irrational. Feelings are feelings; they aren't logical. Water signs can't be reasoned with, as emotions are not intellectual concepts. But that doesn't make them inferior. Water signs have gifts like intuition and imagination.

Cancerians are probably the people you find most frustrating to deal with. The Libra/Cancer relationship is often fraught with problems. They're a moody lot, crabby too. Yet you have a fair bit in common. They are gentle souls like you. The only real difference is that their choices are based on how they feel, while you rely on what you think. Cancerians can teach you a great deal about the human heart.

Pisceans will drive you mad too, because they don't seem to have a brain at all! But oddly enough, although you don't understand them, you can see how they care deeply for others and they also share your interest in the arts.

Sometimes you find it difficult to come to terms with spiritual concepts and the nature of the human psyche. Water signs can teach you about these deep subjects too. They can show you how to see inside yourself.

Water signs will often ask you what you are feeling. You don't know how to answer this question because you operate according to thoughts and ideas, not emotions.

Water signs will often ask you what you are feeling. You don't know how to answer this question because you operate according to thoughts and ideas, not emotions.

Libra is the only sign with an inanimate object, the scales, as a symbol. This makes you highly civilised, rational and conscious. You live totally in your head. But it is by opening your heart that you find the soul union that you are seeking. Your water sign friends can show you how to really connect with people, which is the first step.

Because Scorpio follows Libra you think Scorpios are too intense, too passionate, and too full-on. Scorpios desire real intimacy and depth and that really scares you. For one thing, Scorpios are secretive. They don't communicate openly, not about themselves anyway. But they want to know all about you. It's painful. It feels like you're in a subterranean cave being probed by aliens. Scorpios force you to take a deep, long look at yourself.

When you start to see who you really are, you can begin to form deeper connections with people and experience true intimacy based on shared passions.

But this is scary territory for you. Scorpio's ruling planet, Pluto, is way off in the darkest reaches of space. You can't see it, scientists aren't sure how to categorise it, but it is still there. It's dark and mysterious, and like plutonium, potentially dangerous. It really seems much safer not to go anywhere near this place they call the Underworld.

If you're honest, you'll admit that you need to face your fears about emotions. Allow Scorpios to guide you through the Underworld, for they want to help.

Don't worry, expressing your feelings and finding out what you are passionate about doesn't mean you will suddenly turn into a water sign. To some extent you'll resist them because reasoning and logic are more natural to you than feelings and emotions.

Remember that Venus, and therefore Libra, has a dark side too. Jealousy and revenge, greed and indulgence are some of her less admirable traits.

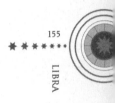

★ ★ ★ ★ ★ ★ ★

LIBRA

If you pretend you don't have a dark side, you either force it underground or project it onto others. Then it becomes more powerful and you will encounter it more frequently in the people you meet. Remember that the Underworld also contains unseen riches that can replenish your heart and soul.

TIPS FOR LIBRA

Ω   Keep a dream diary and learn the language of the unconscious.
Ω   Recognise that there is no light without dark, nor dark without light.
Ω   Every so often spend some time alone, even if you don't want to.
Ω   Recognise there are deeper things beneath surface impressions.
Ω   When you can't make a decision, ask yourself how you really feel.
Ω   Study psychology or astrology.
Ω   Consider the advice of the water signs you meet.

YOUR GIFT TO THE WORLD

How you can make a real difference

Your special gift to the world is your exceptional talent in bringing people together in a spirit of cooperation. If the world were populated only by Librans, planet Earth would be a heavenly paradise. Everyone would be able to see all sides of a problem and work out amicable settlements, so war would be a thing of the past. Everyone would share the Earth's resources in equal measure, and there would be justice for all.

While you probably do need to learn more about feelings, emotions and the deeper undercurrents of life, your real gift is to show others how they can live together in peace and harmony.

FAMOUS PERSONALITIES WITH THE SUN IN LIBRA INCLUDE:

Truman Capote
Jimmy Carter
Matt Damon
Michael Douglas
F. Scott Fitzgerald
Bob Geldof
Mahatma Gandhi
Julia Gillard
George Gershwin
John Lennon
Arthur Miller
Martina Navratilova

Olivia Newton-John
Gwyneth Paltrow
Christopher Reeve
Susan Sarandon
Sting
Margaret Thatcher
Ian Thorpe
Naomi Watts
Sigourney Weaver
Oscar Wilde
Kate Winslet
Catherine Zeta Jones

SCORPIO

24 OCTOBER–22 NOVEMBER

'I shut my eyes and all the world drops dead; I lift
my eyes and all is born again.'
SCORPIO, SYLVIA PLATH

YOUR LIFE MISSION

To deeply probe life's eternal mysteries and transcend the unknown. To penetrate and unite with the source of power.

If you are a Scorpio you're a magnetic and passionate person who loves nothing more than exploring the unknown. You might have an interest in psychology, life after death, or the mysteries of tantric sex, but whatever it is, you want to know all about it.

When you become fascinated by something, there is no stopping you. You never give up until you have plumbed the depths of your subject. You are equally compelled to investigate people and their motives.

It's your task to uncover life's secrets and to bring to conscious awareness whatever is unconscious. Since the unconscious is infinitely vast and unknown, yours is not an easy mission, but you really love a challenge.

You are like a deep-sea diver looking for pearls. There are all sorts of creatures at the bottom of the ocean, many we know nothing about, and some are potentially dangerous. Despite the dangers, the unknown holds a compelling fascination for you.

To survive, you must have some measure of control. That way you won't be swallowed up by whatever is lurking down there. Being in control is a matter of self-preservation.

When you become fascinated by something, there is no stopping you.

Yet, ultimately, being in control is really an illusion. No one can control the unconscious, not even you.

Scorpios always seem to be going through intense experiences that seem fated or karmic, which is another reason why you try hard to stay in control.

You don't like to relinquish your power to anyone, unless you know you can trust them completely, and you don't trust easily. You are fully aware what people are capable of; in fact you have a tendency to assume the worst, at times you almost expect it.

The real danger is that this attitude can turn your life into a self-fulfilling prophecy of doom and gloom. If you always think the worst will happen, it probably will, and then you become the victim of your own negative thinking.

You can rise to the most amazing heights, but your fascination with all things deep and dark means that if you are not careful you can be pulled down into a downward spiral of self-destruction.

You need to let go and lighten up. Try to have more fun, relax and just enjoy living. You need to have faith; develop a belief system, a personal life philosophy that helps you make sense of those things you cannot control.

You don't like to relinquish power to anyone, unless you know you can trust them completely, and you don't trust easily.

Ultimately, to have more control over your life and your destiny, and to reach the heights you are capable of attaining, you actually need to stop trying to control everything.

You can improve your life no end if you could find a way to be more optimistic and stop taking everything so seriously.

But how can you be light and free and optimistic when you are plumbing the depths of the Underworld? And how can you stay in control and take things on faith at the same time? Does being deep make it impossible for you to be carefree?

GIFTS FROM THE PAST

If you're a Scorpio it means you have inherited a lifetime of Libran wisdom which taught you about justice. You learned that life is not always fair.

During your Libra sojourn you were introduced to a wide range of people and learned about relationships. Now you want to deepen those connections. You want to relate to others much more intimately and establish lasting emotional connections that will survive no matter what. You seek a union that is eternal and transcends life and death.

What you have already learned

- *A great deal about other people*
- *The importance of partnership*
- *All about justice and injustice*
- *That life is not always fair*
- *To see all sides of a situation*
- *To reveal to others only what you want them to see*
- *To be a keen observer*
- *That on some issues you need to take a stand*

ELEMENTS OF CHARACTER

Your special place in the zodiac

The eighth sign

Scorpio is the eighth sign of the zodiac. The number eight is like the symbol for infinity, the never-ending cycle of birth, death and rebirth.

Your sign gets a lot of bad press. Known as the repository for all the evils of the world, there's much more to Scorpio than sex, death and depravity.

The combination of fixed energy with the water element makes you like an iceberg. We only see about 10 per cent of the real you.

The truth is that as a Scorpio, your primary interest is the mysteries of life. It just happens that these mysteries reside deep in the unconscious, which is also where socially unacceptable behaviour tends to be deposited. Despite this, your instinct rightly tells you the unconscious also contains treasure in the form of sacred knowledge just waiting to be discovered.

Essentially, what you are trying to do is to dig down to these rich gold deposits found in the soul, to find the source of power itself. But this is a difficult job because it means you have to separate the treasure from all the mud and toxic sludge.

Fixed water

Scorpio is a fixed sign so you are powerful, determined, passionate and thorough. The four fixed signs—Taurus, Leo, Scorpio and Aquarius—all possess these qualities, but your sign has an extra measure of intensity. If required, you can push yourself to the absolute limits of human endurance.

All water signs are deep, but your sign is the deepest of all. The combination of fixed energy with water makes you like an iceberg. We only see about 10 per cent of the real you. The rest is hidden beneath the surface. Though you are intrigued by the unknown and want to uncover life's mysteries, you don't like to reveal your own secrets because you don't like to appear vulnerable.

YOUR GODS AND MYTHS

Topics like astrology and psychology hold a deep fascination for many Scorpios for these are some of the tools that can help you dig beneath the surface. You want to understand more about yourself, the world around you and the people you encounter along the way.

Mars and Pluto are your gods. Both are powerful gods known for their qualities of masculine strength, but Scorpio is actually a feminine sign of the zodiac, so you are a mix of yang and yin.

The truth is that you are equally sensitive and strong.

Having two such dynamic gods makes you incredibly strong in mind and spirit, but underneath there's a soft soul that is very sensitive.

The truth is you are equally sensitive and strong. People often think you are stronger than you really are, but this is exactly the image you like to project; in fact you go out of your way to encourage this belief.

Pluto—Lord of the Underworld

The idea that your sign is somehow associated with the devil is misplaced. As a Scorpio, you know that it's often the person who accuses others of evil deeds who is the real evil doer. In fact the word 'devil' comes from a source that means 'to accuse'.[1]

When the sun is shining and everyone is enjoying life, when there is abundance all around, you may instead be feeling a deep sense of sadness and loss.

Pluto/Hades was the lord of the Underworld who ruled the souls of the dead. He had a magic helmet of invisibility. Just like Pluto, you like to be incognito.

For a long time Pluto lived alone in his Underworld until one day he saw the beautiful Proserpina/Persephone as she was innocently picking flowers. Instantly, he fell in love. He abducted her and took her to live with him. He was no longer alone.

But Persephone's mother, Ceres/Demeter[2], the goddess of grain and fertility, was inconsolable. She missed her daughter so much she caused a great famine.

But as famine spread, Jupiter/Zeus was forced to intervene. An agreement was reached where Persephone would spend part of the year with her mother and the other part with her husband.

This myth is associated with the cycles of the seasons. In autumn and winter, the land is barren, this is when Ceres is unhappy, but Pluto is content because his partner is by his side. In spring and summer Ceres is reunited with her daughter and the land becomes fertile again, but when there is light and abundance, Pluto is left alone in his Underworld.

> *When it comes to relationships, you want a complete union. The attachment is forever as far as you are concerned.*

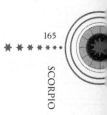

This story resonates deeply with many Scorpios, for when the sun is shining and everyone is enjoying life, when there is abundance all around, you may instead be feeling a deep sense of sadness and loss.

When it comes to relationships, you want a complete union. The attachment is forever as far as you are concerned, but as this story shows, you can no more control others than you can control the seasons.

This story also reminds you there is one god more powerful than yours, Jupiter, and Jupiter rules Sagittarius, the sign that follows Scorpio. Though your sign is possibly the most powerful in the entire zodiac, Sagittarians can teach you even more.

Mars—God of war

Since Pluto was discovered, some astrologers use Pluto as your planetary ruler, some stick with Mars, and some use both.

Mars[3] brings to Aries and Scorpio strength, passion and energy; but Scorpio and Aries differ in that Aries is more open and direct while you are secretive and intense.

There is a mystical aspect to the sexual act that
fascinates you.

When you see the object of your desires, you are magnetically attracted. You know that sex is the gateway to passion, ecstasy and intimacy. There's a mystical aspect to the sexual act that fascinates you.

Mars/Ares and Venus/Aphrodite were secret lovers. When Venus's husband, Vulcan/Hephaestus, heard about his wife's affair, he was determined to expose the lovers and fashioned a net to catch them in the act. He invited all the gods to witness the scene and mock the lovers. When they were discovered, Mars fled the scene. Likewise you prefer to keep your intimate moments private.

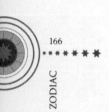
WHAT YOUR PLANETS REVEAL ABOUT YOU

A few years ago astronomers downgraded Pluto from planet to dwarf planet. Given Pluto's symbolic and mythic power, this was probably a bad move. Pluto rules fate and karma; don't we have enough bad karma in the world already without adding to the problem?

And yet there's a positive side too and it's important to look on the bright side whenever you can.

The good news is that when they downgraded Pluto, they also upgraded Ceres from asteroid to dwarf planet, which means that Ceres and Pluto are now on equal footing. This is exactly what happened in the myth.

Pluto is a long way away and it's small, but that
doesn't mean it isn't powerful. As every Scorpio knows,
size really doesn't matter.

As far as astrologers are concerned, Pluto is still a planet, just like the Sun and the Moon are also called planets. How we categorise planets, moons or asteroids in no way effects their energy and mythic power.

Pluto is a long way away and it's small, but that doesn't mean it isn't powerful. As every Scorpio knows, size really doesn't matter.

Pluto was discovered in 1930 at the time of the Great Depression. Pluto has three moons, Charon, Nix and Hydra. Charon was discovered in 1978, and was named for the ferryman who transported the souls of the dead across the river Styx. Nix and Hydra were found in 2005 by the Hubble telescope. NASA's space probe, *New Horizons*, is currently en route to visit Pluto and its satellites. It's due to arrive there in July 2015.[4]

WHAT MAKES YOU TICK?

When you were born it was probably obvious to your parents that you were no ordinary baby. Perhaps your mother had a difficult time in childbirth, or the event was in some other way more memorable than a normal birth. Perhaps you struggled to make it into the world. For many Scorpios themes of birth and death often go hand in hand.

Chances are that even as a child you didn't like your privacy encroached upon. Maybe you kept your bedroom door locked and had a secret hiding place where you would keep your favourite possessions.

Scorpios have a natural curiosity about sex from an early age.

Scorpios have a natural curiosity about sex from an early age. A friend recently told me how she inadvertently walked in on her Scorpio son and his Libran girlfriend when they were in his bedroom. There's nothing very unusual in this except at the time they were only four years old and both stark naked.

Scorpio children like to investigate things for themselves. They can spend hours and hours concentrating on whatever holds their interest.

Perhaps you had to endure a difficult childhood. Many Scorpios are introduced to painful events early in life. These encounters set the scene for your journey ahead.

Anything hidden or unknown fascinates you and you want to get to the bottom of it.

For many Scorpios life is about climbing out of a dark place and into the light. From the outset you have the uncanny knack of being able to alter your course and turn your life around.

Whatever your early circumstances might have been, you soon learned that attack is the best form of defence.

People have a tendency to project onto Scorpios their own disowned traits such as jealousy, resentment, greed and a host of other nasty characteristics. At times you might be on the receiving end of these projections. But as you get older you'll become stronger and learn how to deal with these shadows. You're a survivor.

Scorpio Marie Curie was fascinated by magnetism and was known for her exceptional concentration. Eventually she began studying pitchblende, the ore from which uranium is extracted. She noticed that once the uranium was removed, the pitchblende was still radioactive, and so she began looking for the source of this radioactivity. After years of research, she identified two new elements, polonium and radium. She won two Nobel prizes, one for physics and one for chemistry.

Scorpios can soar to the greatest heights imaginable.

Essentially, there are three types of Scorpios, and each represents a level of soul development.

The lowest level is the scorpion; these are poisonous creatures that hide under rocks, always ready to attack. They are victims of their own negativity and resentment.

Then there are the serpents, many of whom are fascinated by the mysteries of life and in one way or another dedicate themselves to uncovering its secrets. Most Scorpios are somewhere within this level of soul development, for this is a long journey with many twists and turns.

The highest level is the eagle. Here, Scorpios can soar to the greatest heights imaginable.

Your journey in life is about moving towards the great heights where eagles fly.

You possess an incredible capacity for self-control and immense willpower so you can overcome any obstacle that comes your way. Yet it remains a challenge for you to use your power wisely.

One way to do this is to investigate the underlying causes of any problem or mystery. Scorpios have a real instinct for uncovering the truth. This makes you suited for a career in research, psychiatry or psychology, or indeed any occupation where you can use your amazing powers of concentration. You would make an excellent forensic detective. Many doctors and healers are born under your sign, too.

Anything hidden or unknown fascinates you and you want to get to the bottom of it. Like Marie Curie, you will doggedly pursue your objective until it is reached, regardless of the potential danger involved.

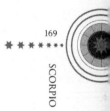

You possess an incredible capacity for self-control and immense willpower so you can overcome any obstacle that comes your way.

You understand and accept that to achieve anything worthwhile, sacrifices must be made. You're completely fearless—nothing fazes you.

There's a fine line between life and death, so you don't waste time on non-essentials. You take life seriously, sometimes too seriously, but you always concentrate on what is really important.

The law of karma is something all Scorpios intrinsically understand. What goes around comes back around, and for Scorpios this often happens more immediately than for other signs.

Like snakes that periodically shed their skin to make way for new growth, you also need to throw off parts of yourself when they are no longer necessary, so that further development can take place.

For many Scorpios life is about climbing out of a dark place and into the light.

Sometimes, just when you are on the verge of reaching a pinnacle in life, events beyond your control can plunge you into a painful, dark place. It may seem as though you are looking into an abyss, but actually this is a signal to shed something before you can move forward and start afresh.

When you find yourself in a dark place, it's worth remembering that these experiences often serve a purpose in the wider context of your soul development, but sometimes the purpose only becomes apparent at a later time.

Life is often bittersweet. Nobody understands this better than you. But even when you are at your lowest ebb, you have deep reserves of strength and the capacity to turn things around.

It might take a whole lifetime, or even many lifetimes, to rise up to the place where eagles soar, but this is where you are ultimately headed.

When you trust enough to totally surrender, you find the deepest fulfilment possible.

There's only one mythic god more powerful than Pluto, and that's Jupiter the sky god, and he rules Sagittarius, the sign that comes after yours. Though you might not realise it, it's Sagittarians who can teach you to fly like an eagle.

THE REALLY IMPORTANT
THINGS IN YOUR LIFE

Power and passion

More than anything, your primary need is for power. You need to find it, then you need to own it, and then you need to find a way to transcend it.

Whatever your specific ambitions in life might be, you know that you can get what you want through perseverance. If required, you'll work at it night and day, year after year, until your objective is reached.

Success brings not just power but usually money. More than any other sign you know that money can corrupt, but you know it can be put to good use as well. It's your attitude towards money and what you do with it that really counts.

You have a great instinct for knowing where to invest your hard-earned cash, but just as with other aspects of your life, you can experience financial highs and lows. Yours can be a journey from rags to riches, or even riches to rags, but always you can rise up from the ashes like a phoenix.

In order to achieve anything worthwhile, you know sacrifices must be made.

There's an aura around you which seems to magnetically attract people who are on the threshold of change. Often you act as an agent or catalyst for their transformation.

Sometimes you draw people to you who seem to want to undermine you and thwart your every move. You may find yourself pitted against others in power struggles. These challenges make you stronger.

As your power and influence grows, you may find that all of a sudden your power is taken away from you. You might, for example, be accused of having a secret motive or a hidden agenda, or even wrongly accused of an evil deed.

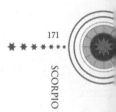

This is another reason why you like to get to the bottom of things, for you need to understand others' motives as well as your own inner drives. It can be a matter of survival.

These kind of fated events are common themes for your sign, for you must continually renew and regenerate yourself in order to grow. Endings are a necessary part of your life, a process you must experience for growth to take place.

It's almost as if you have to undergo certain trials before anyone else. These experiences forge within you a rare depth of understanding and insight into people and life that helps you illuminate the way forward for others to follow. This is why so many therapists, counsellors and healers are born under your sign.

It's fairly common for Scorpios to attract wounded people. This is because they instinctively sense you have a capacity for deep understanding and can help turn their lives around.

While you like to project an ultra-cool and professional aura, deep down you are a passionate and intense person who truly needs both intimacy and privacy.

It's a fine line between venting your feelings and keeping them under wraps. Although you long to share yourself fully and completely with another, you still don't like to surrender your secrets, but at the same time this is exactly what you must eventually do. When you trust enough to totally surrender, you find the deepest fulfilment possible.

When strong emotions such as grief stir you, your power is transcended and you can be touched by another person at the very deepest part of your soul.

This kind of soul union and emotional intimacy is possible when you let go and express what you are truly feeling.

When those intense emotions that simmer just below the surface flood in, your iceberg starts to melt and you flow into the ocean. You become part of something much larger, and join with the source you have been seeking all along.

SHARING YOUR KNOWLEDGE

How you get along with others

People you can teach:	Air signs—Gemini, Libra, Aquarius
Compatible similar signs:	Water signs—Cancer, Scorpio, Pisces
Compatible complementary signs:	Earth signs—Taurus, Virgo, Capricorn
People you can learn from:	Fire signs—Aries, Leo, Sagittarius

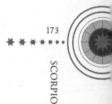

Relating to air signs (Gemini, Libra, Aquarius)

Once you solve a mystery or uncover the truth, you want to enlighten those who will benefit from this knowledge. The people who need your insight most of all are the air signs. These people understand virtually nothing about feelings or emotions, let alone the unconscious.

Because the air signs are elusive and flit about on the surface like Persephone picking flowers, you want to abduct them and take them into your Underworld. You want to show them that there is much more to life than what is on the surface. But frankly air signs are terrified of anything deep and meaningful and therefore avoid getting close to you, for they prefer to keep things light and breezy.

Air signs are elusive and flit about on the surface; you want to show them there is much more to life.

Because air signs live in their heads, not their hearts, they run a mile whenever you try to get close to them. They're totally out of their depth.

In spite of the fact that air signs are, to your way of thinking, superficial, flighty and elusive, you make an extra effort to connect with them. You want them to reveal themselves to you, but this is unlikely to ever happen. Air and water is the most challenging of all relationship combinations—partly why you find them so alluring.

Relating to water signs (Cancer, Scorpio, Pisces)

When your water sign friends need a shoulder to cry on, they usually turn to you. Although you don't usually show others how vulnerable you are, you're more likely to open up to your water sign friends than anyone else. You know your secrets are safe here.

> *When your water sign friends need a shoulder to cry on, they usually turn to you.*

Cancerians and Pisceans are sensitive souls, just like you. They are seeking an emotional and spiritual connection, a real soul union.

Water signs provide you with emotional support when you need it most, but sometimes it can all get a bit too emotional. For when there is too much water, there is always the risk that someone might drown.

Relationships with other Scorpios can be intense to say the least. When two Scorpios get together, neither is willing to relinquish their power; and yet that is exactly what is required for growth to occur. In these powerful encounters, one Scorpio might become an eagle, while the other can regress into a scorpion, secretly undermining the power of the other.

But in all Scorpio relationships the potential exists for a creative and transforming union where great achievements and profound insights are possible.

Relating to earth Signs (Taurus, Virgo, Capricorn)

With the probable exception of Taurus, which is your opposite sign, earth signs are an excellent match for you. Both Virgos and Capricorns accept you for who you are. Scorpio, Virgo and Capricorn are the three most maligned signs of the zodiac, in that all have had negative associations of one kind or another thrust upon them. You understand they have secret depths not many people see.

Both Virgos and Capricorns accept you for who you are.

Consequently, you share a real feeling of compassion for each other and a deep mutual understanding. Earth and water combine well because earth is able to contain water and gives it a firm base, while water nurtures and nourishes the earth, making it fertile and rich.

Taurus, the other earth sign, is a fixed sign like you, and because it's your opposite sign this relationship can be highly creative. But it can also be destructive and incredibly painful, because neither of you is willing to compromise.

Relating to fire signs (Aries, Leo, Sagittarius)

People born under the fire signs will constantly challenge you, but if you can learn to trust them, they can teach you more about yourself than you ever thought possible. They can even show you how to reach the heights of the eagle.

What fire signs have and you don't is the ability to bounce back and remain positive, no matter what. They always look on the bright side.

While you are in touch with the underlying forces that sustain life, you often lose sight of the positive experiences that make life worthwhile. You have trouble accepting things on faith. What they have and you don't is the ability to bounce back and remain positive no matter what. They assume the best while you usually assume the worst. They always look on the bright side. But they can't possibly be happy all the time, can they?

Because you don't trust easily, you're often suspicious of fire signs. You might question their motives, but these people are here to help you evolve.

WHAT YOU NEED TO LEARN

Trust and faith

Apparently, it's not true that scorpions will sting themselves to death, but when surrounded by a ring of fire, they become highly agitated and die because they feel trapped and cannot escape.

This is just how you can react when you encounter people born under the fire element, because fire signs force you to evolve, and that involves some kind of death experience, something that is beyond your control. Someone else has the power.

When you stare into an abyss, you need a positive and optimistic person to come along and lift you up.

It can be really difficult for you to have faith and develop trust, but these are the character ingredients you most need to acquire.

The problem is that you take life far too seriously. At some point you might begin to wonder what it would be like to have more fun, but somehow people who are always having fun seem so superficial.

Literally and figuratively, being 'up' is not a comfortable feeling for you. 'Down' is much more natural.

But in order to become an eagle, to take the next step in your personal soul development, you need to learn how to fly and enjoy being 'up'. Fire signs can help you, but this involves a leap of faith on your part.

It's the same with air travel. Lots of Scorpios don't like flying. Your nervousness is due to the lack of control you have at 35 000 feet. It's okay when you're in control, when you are in the driver's seat, but if you're the passenger, you become nervous—not that you usually let on.

In your darkest moments, everything can seem pointless. When you stare into an abyss, you need a positive and optimistic person to come along and lift you up. The trouble is you don't like to admit to anyone that you need help. It's tough for you to reach out to others because you don't like to appear vulnerable.

Sagittarians can provide you with the sense of purpose and meaning you have been looking for. Best of all, they can make you laugh and help you look on the bright side.

TAKING THE NEXT STEP

You can learn a lot from Sagittarians and the other fire signs. These people are spontaneous and are eager to encourage you. Just as you want the air signs to get in touch with their emotions, the fire signs want to help you to be more positive, outgoing and spontaneous.

You may not realise it, but you have more in common with fire signs than you think. Like you, they're passionate, imaginative and creative. Fire signs stir you up. Fire makes water boil and because you are made of ice, when you are around them you quickly start to melt, you lose control, you're transformed and it's unsettling to say the least.

Sagittarians are spontaneous and incredibly carefree. They never seem to have any problems. How can life be that simple?

Aries people are just as passionate as you and yet they wear their heart on their sleeve. Why do they do that? Because they're comfortable revealing their feelings. They can show you how.

Leo is a fixed sign like you, so this can be a difficult relationship because fixed signs are like leopards that don't change their spots.

But Leos are ruled by the Sun, so when you are in a dark place they can bring you back towards the light.

The essential reason that Sagittarians cause you so much angst is that they simply cannot be controlled. For them, freedom is essential, so when you encounter them, you can't use the same tactics as with everyone else. When you try to harness and tame them, they slip out of your grasp and just gallop away without a care in the world. They can be infuriating.

They just accept that everything will turn out for the best and magically it does! Even when life takes an unexpected turn they just take it in their stride.

They never seem to have any problems. How can life be that simple? Do they have some kind of trick that you don't know about? What is it?

Admit it. There are some things that can only be explained by faith. As you mature you will come to acknowledge that you can indeed learn something from the fire signs.

Just because you open up to being enlightened by Sagittarians and other fire signs doesn't mean you have to relinquish your power. Actually, your power grows when you learn to take things on trust. Then you can unite with ultimate power, the creative power of the universe.

TIPS FOR SCORPIO

♏ Have faith in the universe.
♏ Develop more trust by revealing a secret about yourself.
♏ Keep an open mind about different beliefs and philosophies.
♏ Realise that being in control is an illusion.
♏ Now and then take a long flight to a new holiday destination.
♏ Every so often laugh, or cry, or let others see how you truly feel.
♏ Consider the advice of the fire signs you meet.

YOUR GIFT TO THE WORLD

How you can make a real difference

Your special gift to the world is your x-ray vision. If everyone born on Earth was a Scorpio, we could not hide from the truth about ourselves. The human race would soon stop the endless cycle of karmic debt, because we would all have to own up to our role in the evils of the world. No longer would we be playing the broken record called the 'blame game'.

Although you need to learn to have a little more faith and to look on the bright side more often, your true gift is to make people face up to themselves.

In following your mission to explore all that is hidden, you help transform the world by eliminating everything that is no longer needed, and in doing so, you bring to the world an eternally renewable power resource, a fresh creative opportunity for a new start in life.

FAMOUS PERSONALITIES
WITH THE SUN IN SCORPIO
INCLUDE:

Marie Antoinette	Indira Gandhi
Dr Christian Barnard	Bill Gates
John Cleese	Grace Kelly
Hillary Clinton	Robert Kennedy
Christopher Columbus	K.D. Lang
Captain James Cook	Vivien Leigh
Marie Curie	Charles Manson
Danny DeVito	Pablo Picasso
Leonardo Dicaprio	Sylvia Plath
Sally Field	Julia Roberts
Larry Flynt	Robert Louis Stevenson
Jodie Foster	Voltaire

SAGITTARIUS

23 NOVEMBER–22 DECEMBER

'Life would be infinitely happier if we could
only be born at the age of eighty and gradually
approach eighteen.'

SAGITTARIUS, MARK TWAIN

YOUR LIFE MISSION

To seek the truth and a sense of meaning and purpose. To experience the world and live life to the full.

As a Sagittarian you want to experience everything there is to experience. Life is an incredible adventure. You are on a quest to find ultimate meaning and a sense of purpose, but you want to have fun along the way.

As far as you're concerned, life is for living. In undertaking the quest for your own personal grail, whatever it may be, you're not really interested in the objective; it's the journey itself that matters most.

Complete freedom of movement is essential to you, so anyone who tries to harness you, or break you in, is to be avoided at all costs.

Your mission is to explore the world and experience everything you can. Above all, yours is a journey of the spirit, and your spirit is free. Freedom is like oxygen—without enough of it, you fail to thrive.

You're completely fearless and incredibly optimistic. Your sign is the luckiest sign of the zodiac and because you expect to succeed, you usually do.

But what often happens is that you run into obstacles and restrictions that frustrate you no end. You simply can't bear to be tied down or limited in any way. You are the archer, aiming outwards and upwards; always shooting towards your target.

Red tape, rules and obligations are some of the hurdles you stumble to jump over. As you gallop along, you love the natural causeways, the rivers and hills you traverse, but man-made obstacles can trip you up.

Complete freedom is essential to you, so anyone who tries to harness you, or break you in, is to be avoided at all costs.

*You're completely fearless and incredibly optimistic.
Your sign is the luckiest sign of the zodiac. Because you
expect to succeed, you usually do.*

However, you're only half horse; your top half is human. You're actually a centaur and the human part of you has to live in the real world where responsibilities cannot be avoided.

The world is full of systems and regulations. Civilisation would not function without them, and though you don't care to admit it, you actually need these rules.

While the horse part of you wants to be free, the human part must face reality.

So how can you remain free and unfettered and at the same time jump over the hurdles always put in front of you? How can you cope with the restrictions placed on your freedom? Is it possible for you to be a spiritual person while living in a material world, and still fulfil your purpose?

GIFTS FROM THE PAST

If you are a Sagittarius you have inherited a lifetime of Scorpio wisdom. Scorpio made you strong and passionate. You have emerged from the Underworld so you can survive just about anything; you feel invincible. Whatever happens, you always manage to bounce back and hold onto your faith in life.

What you have already learned

⊛ *That you are incredibly strong*
⊛ *That you can rely on your instinct and intuition*
⊛ *How to survive just about anything*
⊛ *That there is a fine line between life and death*
⊛ *To own your own power*

- *To seek the truth*
- *That honesty is the best policy*
- *That life is short and should therefore be lived to the full*

SECRETS OF THE ZODIAC

ELEMENTS OF CHARACTER

Your special place in the zodiac

The ninth sign

Sagittarius is the ninth sign of the zodiac and one sign away from the tenth sign, where potentially, we can attain our goals in life.

Before this stage can be reached, it's necessary to know where we are going, which is what your sign is most interested in. You are seeking a target and taking aim. You want to know what lies ahead of you. You are looking for your purpose in life.

You are a free-spirit and you live your life accordingly.

With a broad expansive vision, you want to soar high and see the world and find your inspiration.

Placed between Scorpio and Capricorn, signs that see the serious side of life, you are much more interested in having fun. Why be glum and sad? Life should be enjoyed and lived to the full, no matter what. You are a free spirit and you live your life accordingly.

Mutable fire

Sagittarius is a mutable sign, which makes you highly versatile. All four mutable signs—Gemini, Virgo, Sagittarius and Pisces—are adaptable and rather restless, because when the Sun is in these signs, the seasons are changing.

With the possible exception of Gemini, Sagittarius is the most changeable sign of all, because your mutability is combined with the spontaneity of the fire element.

The mix of mutability and fire explains why you are always on the go. You leap about from place to place, and sometimes you accidentally start spot fires.

The fire element makes you energetic, creative and dynamic, but there are different types of fire. Your type of fire expression is like a forest fire that can easily flare up and change direction. Sometimes it's necessary for the forest to burn, so that new growth can occur, but things can quickly get out of hand. It all depends on what type of fuel is burning and the prevailing weather conditions.

The mix of mutability and fire explains why you are always on the go. You leap about from place to place, and sometimes you can accidentally start spot fires.

YOUR GODS AND MYTHS

There's a large part of you that wants to discover how the universe operates. This has something to do with your last sojourn in Scorpio where your soul plumbed the depths of the unconscious.

Having some kind of belief system is essential to your spiritual wellbeing.

Now you are seeking spiritual enlightenment. Some Sagittarians are drawn to organised religion, others adhere to their own brand of faith, and some chop and change their life philosophy as often as they make new friends.

Having a belief system is essential to your spiritual wellbeing. It doesn't matter what form it takes, for you know the most important thing is to keep an open mind.

Jupiter—Supreme sky god

Jupiter/Zeus, the youngest son of Saturn/Cronus, overthrew his tyrant father to become the all-powerful sky god.

Jupiter fell in love with and married his sister Juno/Hera, but he was constantly unfaithful to his wife.

To escape detection, he would often change himself into a variety of animals, but no sooner had he made love to a new goddess, nymph or mortal, than he would immediately lose interest and go looking for his next sexual conquest.

Jupiter's relationship with his wife was turbulent to say the least, yet they stayed together and through it all retained their sense of humour.

Like Jupiter, you too can be a bit of a Don Juan. You really don't like to be tied down. Any kind of restriction makes you pull at the reins. But despite your restlessness, it is possible for you to make a life-long commitment.

Saturn governs the responsibilities that come with maturity, but like Jupiter, you want to overthrow Saturn. You see restrictions as major obstacles to your freedom.

You are the archetypal youngest son, always young at heart. But when you rise to a position of authority, there are responsibilities you must face. Learning how to take personal responsibility is one of your most important lessons in life.

Chiron—Wise healer and teacher

Centaurs were also descendants of Saturn/Cronus. Most centaurs were wild and unruly creatures. Aggressive and indulgent, they spent most of their time cavorting in drunken orgies, all except the wise Chiron, who was a teacher, healer and musician.

Chiron educated a number of heroes including Hercules, who was his friend. One day Hercules took aim at a herd of savage centaurs, but his poison arrow accidentally pierced Chiron's thigh.

The poison caused Chiron to suffer in dreadful agony, but because he was part mortal and part immortal, he couldn't die. Although he was a great healer, he wasn't able to heal himself.

Chiron symbolises your capacity for wisdom and your skills in the arts, teaching and music.

Eventually, Chiron appealed to Zeus to be released from his suffering and was given permission to die and enter the Underworld.

Chiron symbolises your capacity for wisdom and your skills in the arts, teaching and music.

On some level your journey is about accepting the challenge to rise above the level of the ordinary centaur and become a wise Chiron. Doing so means you must pay the price of experiencing pain. This is the pain of being human.

WHAT YOUR PLANETS REVEAL ABOUT YOU

Jupiter is by far the largest planet in our solar system, apart from the Sun of course. Jupiter is vast. All the other planets would easily fit inside Jupiter twice over, with room to spare. A day on Jupiter is less than ten hours long. Apart from the Moon and Venus, Jupiter is the brightest object in the night sky. It takes 12 years to move through the zodiac, spending around 12 months in each sign.

Like Jupiter, you are larger than life and move about quite rapidly. You see the big picture and wide open spaces appeal to you. You live life in the fast lane.

'Jovial' is a word derived from Jupiter, and it describes you very well. You are naturally happy, optimistic and fun to be around.

Like Jupiter, you are larger than life and move about quite rapidly. You see the big picture and wide open spaces appeal to you. You live life in the fast lane.

On 7 January 1610, Galileo discovered Jupiter's four largest moons: Ganymede, Io, Europa and Callisto. Ganymede is the largest moon in the solar system, it's even bigger than Mercury. Astronomers continue to discover moons in orbit around Jupiter, at last count there were 63[1], including a number of captured asteroids. The Jupiter system is like a solar system in miniature.

Named after the wise healer, Chiron was discovered in 1977, heralding the re-emergence of natural healing and alternative medicine. Chiron orbits between Saturn and Uranus and takes 50 years to move around the Sun. Often it's not until the age of 50 that Sagittarians are ready to leave youth behind. It's then they start to develop more maturity and wisdom.

WHAT MAKES YOU TICK?

As a child you were probably always falling out of trees and coming home with cuts and scratches, or maybe you wouldn't come home at all. Growing up you may have had your fair share of broken bones and sport injuries, and loved every moment of it.

Your parents may have tried to keep you on a short leash, if not an actual harness, so you wouldn't run off, but it probably didn't work.

No doubt you were a playful, happy kid with an insatiable curiosity about people and the world. This curiosity never leaves you. You are constantly on the lookout for your next adventure.

> *Making people laugh is as easy as falling off a log, and you're good at that too.*

Even before you hear of a greener pasture, you gallop off to look for one. It doesn't matter how far away it is, or whether or not you know how to get there, or even if it exists.

Your natural curiosity about life can take you on a long journey towards personal enlightenment, but you don't take life too seriously because you want to enjoy the ride.

> *You think that if something is good, then more of it must be better.*

You delight in telling people about your amazing adventures and these stories can turn into tall tales, for you are prone to exaggerate. Every time you tell a story, it can become grander and more dramatic, until it turns into an epic myth.

Though you can exaggerate and embellish a story for effect, this doesn't mean you are dishonest—far from it. Your sign is perhaps the most honest, straightforward and open sign of the zodiac. You never mince words; you come right out with it.

Sagittarians are known to suffer from foot-in-mouth disease. If someone asks for your honest opinion, as far as you are concerned they should be prepared to hear it. 'Yes, your bum does look big in that' is just a statement of fact. Why should people get upset?

You aren't the most diplomatic person on the planet, but isn't it refreshing in this day and age, with so much spin and political correctness, to hear the plain and honest truth?

You're a great comedian. Making people laugh is as easy as falling off a log, and you're good at that too.

During his life, Sagittarian writer and humorist Mark Twain travelled widely. His enormous body of work included many travel features. Many of Twain's best-loved books are adventure stories, such as *The Adventures of Tom Sawyer* and *The Adventures of Huckleberry Finn*. His biographer, Albert Bigelow Pain, noted how Twain was a highly spiritual man: 'Mark Twain's God was of colossal proportions—so vast, indeed, that the constellated stars were but molecules in His veins—a God as big as space itself.'[2]

In 1909, Twain said, 'I came in with Halley's Comet in 1835. It is coming again next year (1910), and I expect to go out with it. It will be the greatest disappointment of my life if I don't...'[3] He was not disappointed.

There are three reasons you are accident-prone. First, you have an adventurous nature; second, you tend to overestimate your ability to do things; and third, you don't manage the material world very well.

Even when accidents do happen, which for you can be fairly frequently, there often turns out to be a fringe benefit attached. At the very least you have another really interesting story to tell.

Your intuition is highly developed, though you can sometimes misinterpret signals. Maybe when that attractive stranger winked at you last week, they really just had some dust in their eye—but as it turned out, you really hit it off.

You have horse sense. Call it instinct or intuition;
you have this uncanny ability to sense what is just
around the corner.

Speaking of your personal relationships, for one thing, you get bored easily, so there has to be some variety, and not just in the bedroom. You have a tendency to run a mile when you sense your current love interest is looking for a permanent commitment, because freedom to come and go is vital.

As you get older you might begin to wonder if you will ever settle down, after all, it's the one experience you are still yet to have, but you always seem to put it off until tomorrow.

You prefer the temporary high to the long-term medium. As the saying goes, live fast, die young and leave a good-looking corpse.[4]

> *'Jovial' is a word derived from Jupiter, and it describes you very well. You are naturally happy, optimistic and fun to be around.*

SAGITTARIUS

Not that you have a death wish—far from it. You love life and are the life of any party. But your natural excitement when combined with stimulants can lead to excesses of all kinds.

You think that if something is good, then more of it must be better. It's probably a good idea therefore to avoid drugs and alcohol, for you are on a natural high already and can have difficulty knowing when you have had enough. Moderation is not a word in the Sagittarian vocabulary. Though you are lucky, this doesn't mean you are immortal, as Sagittarians Jimi Hendrix or Anna Nicole Smith would tell you if they could.

You're high-spirited and always put adventure and fun before duty and responsibility. You act on impulse and take advantage of any opportunity that comes along, and if no opportunity comes, then you look for one.

> *You know that money will turn up when you need it, and magically it does.*

Taking risks is one thing, being totally reckless is quite another. Sometimes you can be too foolhardy for your own good. As you go after your next big thrill, be it fast cars, sky-diving or betting all your money on a good thing in the Melbourne Cup, maybe you are trying to avoid something? Over time thrill-seeking can wear thin. As you mature you will begin to realise that excitement for its own sake can be an empty experience.

What you do have is horse sense. Call it instinct, or intuition; you have this uncanny knack of sensing what is just around the corner.

Just like real horses, you know when danger is about. These instincts help you flee from dangerous predators like those Capricorns who want to rein you in and make you more responsible.

Sagittarians like William Blake, Beethoven and Steven Spielberg are good role models for you—creative, passionate and visionary. You too can rise to great heights, but to achieve lasting success, you need to have discipline. This is where you fall down, at least early in life, before you develop the wisdom that comes from maturity.

Above all, you need autonomy and space.

You're incredibly generous and equally extravagant. This is partly because you don't recognise the true value of money. You'd give away your last dollar to a homeless person, even if you were homeless yourself. You'd spend a month's wages on a night out to say *bon voyage* to your new best friend, who you met last week. As far as you are concerned, money is there to be spent. You know it will turn up when you need it, and magically it does, so it doesn't bother you if you don't have a regular pay cheque.

Being free-spirited, you are definitely not suited to being tied to a desk, nor any routine job where you don't have free rein. Above all, you need autonomy and space.

You might become an actor, a musician or a motivational speaker. You could find happiness as a teacher, priest or spiritual advisor. Since you like to explore the world, your talents might be best employed in the travel sector, such as a flight attendant, pilot or tour guide, or in any kind of outdoors work. Since Sagittarians are often very physically fit and active, you could even achieve success as a professional athlete.

You are young at heart and will probably retain your youthful enthusiasm throughout your life.

At some point though, your restless urges will have all been met, you will have experienced everything you can possibly experience and you'll begin to wonder what comes next. Maybe then you might even consider settling down.

THE REALLY IMPORTANT THINGS IN YOUR LIFE

Experiencing the world and working out what life means

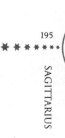

In all you do in life, you are on a spiritual quest for meaning. This quest can take you along many roads.

But you are half human and half horse, so you need to express both parts of yourself. Part of you is spiritual and part is physical. The physical part of you is athletic and muscular like a horse.

Most Sagittarians enjoy keeping fit and most are blessed with excellent metabolism, as Jupiter is the planet that rules the liver. Overindulgence is the one thing you need to watch for. Whether it's too much food, too much alcohol, or even too much exercise, again it comes down to your inability to recognise limitations.

The fittest person I know is a Sagittarian. She's twice as fit as most women half her age. She runs about 10 km every day and that's on top of going to the gym up to five times a week and bushwalking most Sundays. She loves it. It's only recently, since turning 50, that she's starting to be aware of her limits. But that isn't slowing her down.

Sagittarians love to travel. You especially love the great outdoors and being close to nature. Exotic and out of the way destinations intrigue you; visiting ancient temples and experiencing diverse cultures holds a special fascination.

They say travel broadens the mind, but your mind is already broad to begin with, so as you journey to all corners of the globe your mind becomes as large as Jupiter itself. Travel enriches your spirit.

Sagittarians love to travel. You especially love the great outdoors and being close to nature.

When people say the word 'spiritual', you know the true meaning of the word. It doesn't have anything to do with organised religion. Spiritual means 'of the spirit' and spirit is the animating energy within all life. It's this life energy that you seek to express by living life to the full.

Your spiritual quest might start at university where you are exposed to a wide range of people and teachings. Countless subjects like law, theology, astronomy, music, philosophy, sport and languages may interest you.

University life often appeals to Sagittarians, though most prefer to learn from experience rather than from books. Throughout life you'll be exposed to a wide variety of teachings, and you're always looking to expand your horizons and knowledge.

Because your quest is to find your purpose in life, you are likely to become interested in a host of spiritual subjects. In the 1970s it might have been the Hare Krishna movement, today it might be Buddhism, and in the future perhaps Scientology. Any number of esoteric subjects might hold your interest for a time, until you encounter the next really interesting philosophy. Many Sagittarians are looking for a guru.

Traditional religions might also appeal, but you will soon discard any teaching which in your eyes is hypocritical, and you're not likely to become involved in fundamentalist teachings that involve disciplined ritual worship.

Deep down you understand that spirit is simply the energy which animates life. To you, it's quite straightforward. Having been through the Scorpio Underworld, you know that life goes on after death, and this knowledge sets you free.

Even science teaches that energy can't be destroyed, it only changes form. Einstein showed how matter and energy are the same. The material world of matter is composed of the same spirit-energy that you know all about. Once you get your head around this concept, you'll have less trouble dealing with restrictions and red tape because you'll realise that these too are aspects of spirit.

SHARING YOUR KNOWLEDGE

How you get along with others

People you can teach:	Water signs—Cancer, Scorpio, Pisces
Compatible similar signs:	Fire signs—Aries, Leo, Sagittarius
Compatible complementary signs:	Air signs—Gemini, Libra, Aquarius
People you can learn from:	Earth signs—Taurus, Virgo, Capricorn

Relating to water signs (Cancer, Scorpio, Pisces)

Whenever you have a philosophical insight about life, you're eager to share it with anyone and everyone. Most of all you want to educate the water signs. These are the people who lack your natural confidence and optimism and need your encouragement.

All they really need is a more positive outlook and their problems would be solved. To you, they seem withdrawn and sad and unable to help themselves, so you like to cheer them up and give them a helping hand.

Water signs are suspicious of your motives and are
uncomfortable being pushed forward.

The only problem is that water signs are suspicious of your motives and are uncomfortable being pushed forward. They usually resist your encouragement until they get used to the feeling, and that might take a while, and you don't really want to hang around that long. You become impatient and frustrated with their procrastination, but for some reason you always seem drawn to water signs and help them as often as you can.

Relating to fire signs (Aries, Leo, Sagittarius)

Many of your good friends are probably fire signs and that's because you have lots in common. All fire signs are creative, outgoing and confident.

But relationships between fire signs can become ultra-competitive. Too much fire can become destructive and really wild if it gets out of hand, potentially leading to accidents, for all fire signs are risk-takers. When fiery people get together they encourage each other to take bigger risks, which can lead to difficulties if not kept under control.

Relating to air signs (Gemini, Libra, Aquarius)

Relationships with air signs are potentially the happiest relationships you will encounter. Air helps fire to burn. In fact, fire won't burn without air, so the presence of air signs in your life is quite essential.

Air helps fire to burn. In fact, fire won't burn without air, so the presence of air signs in your life can be quite essential.

Librans and Aquarians are excellent matches for you; they ignite your passions. Gemini, however, is your opposite sign. Because opposites are attracted to one another, you might be fascinated by Geminis, but they are very different to you. Air signs think rationally and logically, while you are essentially spiritual and instinctive. You have very different ways of seeing the world. You see the forest while they see the trees. Communication problems can result.

Relating to earth signs (Taurus, Virgo, Capricorn)

People born under the earth signs will restrict your freedom and frustrate you no end, but you can learn a lot from them if only you would realise it. In fact, earth signs can provide you with form and structure to help you to build something lasting and worthwhile.

They are here to show you how you can manage the material world.

Putting down roots is not something you are keen to do because then you feel trapped by obligations and responsibilities.

The enlightenment you are seeking is not always found in some mystical faraway land; it might be right beneath your feet, if you just stood still for a moment and looked a little more closely.

WHAT YOU NEED TO LEARN

Self-discipline

Life wasn't meant to be easy, so the saying goes. What is not easy for you are all those rules and regulations. As far as you're concerned, life would be much easier if everyone did exactly as they pleased.

Whenever you want to do something, some bureaucrat or politician has decided there are forms you have to fill in. You feel like Big Brother is watching your every move and you can't bear it.

You have a great creative idea, but find you have to do paperwork, manage the accounts and deal with the tax man. At every turn you seem to run into obstacles.

Time can be your enemy, because you lack self-discipline and patience.

It seems like someone always comes along and tries to build a fence around your paddock.

You know there are always greener pastures you can graze in and off you gallop. But then the same thing happens all over again. It seems like someone always comes along and tries to build a fence around your paddock.

You can end up repeating the same pattern over and over again, going nowhere fast and then your search for meaning becomes meaningless.

The more you avoid the real world of material reality, where time is money and where rules and personal responsibilities must be adhered to, the further away you are from actually reaching your goals.

Never fear, for the earth signs can show you how to break this cycle and find both purpose and fulfilment. They can help you to develop the discipline to go the distance and stay in one place long enough to build something lasting, to put down roots and reap the long-term rewards.

TAKING THE NEXT STEP

This earth element, with all its focus on details, regulations and time, is the element that frustrates you the most. Fortunately for you, diligent earth souls are eager to help you understand the importance of conservation, moderation and sustained effort. They want to help you create something truly worthwhile that lasts.

Earth signs can help you become more organised so that you can actually reach your goals. Just like you want to help the water signs to be more confident and outgoing, the earth signs are keen to give you practical advice.

Having to live on Earth is difficult for you. Most of the time you feel like a teenager who has been grounded for staying out late, and you're just itching to escape.

While you are busy watching the big screen, the earth signs take it one step further and focus on the pixels. You have vision, but they have common sense. Together you can move mountains.

Although earth signs embody everything you find most frustrating, what you need to realise is that they also have the talents and tools you most need.

Taureans have the financial nous you lack. They can show you how to invest and even save. While you are the luckiest sign of the zodiac, when it comes to luck with money, you actually come in second place to Taurus.

Virgos are mutable like you, but somehow they manage to stay in one place long enough to deal with all the small stuff that you find so irritating. They are good at filling in forms and reading the fine print. Virgos are able to point out all the potential pitfalls that might trip you up. Though you have great foresight and vision, they see these small glitches well before you. If you ignore their advice you will have to suffer the indignity of the look in their eyes that says, 'I told you so'.

If you continually avoid taking personal responsibility, you actually make the problem far bigger. If you dealt with the task at hand right away, in a timely fashion, instead of ignoring it, it wouldn't become a huge issue.

Capricorns embody everything you find most frustrating and annoying.

Goats live on top of mountains, the highest place we can climb. They know this terrain. They have no problem jumping from rock to rock, but this is where horses fear to tread. Goats can show you the route to take to get to the top of the mountain. It's the one place on planet Earth you have yet to explore, all you have to do is follow them.

It's not uncommon for Sagittarians to suffer
from claustrophobia.

Having to live on Earth is difficult for you. Most of the time you feel like a teenager who has been grounded for staying out late, and you're just itching to escape.

Living on Jupiter as you do, which is so vast and majestic, any smaller environment gives you the heebie-jeebies. It's not uncommon for Sagittarians to suffer from claustrophobia. You'd be quite content to explore the universe forever, but eventually you have to come back down to Earth.

Since you're honest you're probably the first to admit you don't handle restrictions very well. As you have an open mind and are always willing to learn new things, why not let the earth signs show you how to manage the material world? They can help you turn your grand vision into a durable lasting reality.

TIPS FOR SAGITTARIUS

- ✗ Recognise the grass is not always greener in the next paddock.
- ✗ Remember the moral of the story of the tortoise and the hare.
- ✗ As an experiment, see what happens if you stay in one place longer than usual.
- ✗ Now and then set yourself a deadline and make an effort to stick to it.
- ✗ Learn to be more patient with yourself.
- ✗ When you become frustrated, realise it's because you lack self-discipline.
- ✗ Consider the advice of the earth signs you meet.

YOUR GIFT TO THE WORLD

How you can make a real difference

Your special gift to the world is your positive attitude and wonderful enthusiasm which inspires people everywhere you go. If everyone on Earth were a Sagittarian, no one would ever be sad, depressed or lonely. There wouldn't be any religious conflict either, for everyone would simply believe in the wondrous spirit of life which is far above any organised religion.

Although you don't manage material reality very well, your real gift is to inspire people everywhere and to live life to the full.

FAMOUS PERSONALITIES WITH THE SUN IN SAGITTARIUS INCLUDE:

Beethoven

William Blake

Billy Connolly

Kirk Douglas

Sammy Davis, Jr

Chris Evert

Jane Fonda

Bob Hawke

Jimi Hendrix

Scarlett Johansson

Bruce Lee

Billie Jean King

Mary, Queen of Scots

Bette Midler

Edith Piaf

Brad Pitt

Keith Richards

Frank Sinatra

Anna Nicole Smith

Britney Spears

Steven Spielberg

Tina Turner

Mark Twain

Frank Zappa

CAPRICORN

23 DECEMBER–20 JANUARY

'The time is always right to do what is right.'
CAPRICORN, MARTIN LUTHER KING, JR

YOUR LIFE MISSION

To lead by example. To act responsibly and with integrity to make the world a better place.

Being a Capricorn is a serious business. Your sign has a lot to do with achievement, and it's not only in your work, for you take a professional approach to everything you do. You're reliable, practical, organised and incredibly driven.

Whatever the task before you, you know how to get the job done. It doesn't matter how long it takes because you have infinite patience. To build something worthwhile takes time and effort, and you have plenty of both.

To achieve the results you want, you know it's vital to have a plan. You are the architect of the zodiac. You like to have a blueprint before you begin. One must lay a firm foundation and most importantly get the right permits; there are rules one must follow.

Every Capricorn has their own particular set of rules; they vary according to individual planetary influences. But whatever your rules turn out to be, you know how important it is to be true to your principles and live with integrity.

Because you're incredibly responsible and self-disciplined, you think these are the most admirable character traits. You want everyone to be just as diligent and principled as you, but very few people are.

To build something worthwhile takes time and effort,
and you have plenty of both.

But as you reliably apply yourself to the task at hand, you invariably encounter people who don't behave according to your rules. They cause disruptions and interfere with your plans, and this affects the ordered way in which the world should function.

SECRETS OF THE ZODIAC

The mavericks, the eccentrics, the rebels of the world—these are some of the people who cause you problems. Then there are those upstarts who refuse to conform or follow rules. Most of all it's people who don't take any personal responsibility for their actions. Don't they realise they're causing problems? People who don't follow the rules really get on your goat.

If others constantly undermine authority, have no sense of duty and ignore the rules, how can you reach your goals and leave the world in better shape than you found it? What's the point of trying to build something worthwhile when people have no appreciation for all your time and effort?

But why should you shoulder all the responsibilities when others don't follow suit? And if you always take on responsibilities on their behalf, aren't you in a way contributing to the problem?

More importantly, what about that free spirit inside you that would really love to escape your self-imposed rules and experience the same creative freedom that others enjoy?

You want everyone to be just as diligent and principled as you, but very few people are.

How is this possible? How can you be free to express yourself when you always have to maintain order? Do you always have to be the one in charge? Does being responsible mean you always have to put duty first?

GIFTS FROM THE PAST

If you're a Capricorn you have inherited a lifetime of Sagittarian wisdom. Sagittarius taught you to find a purpose in life. You found a target at which to aim and you learned to have faith in yourself. Now your goal is to master the material world, not just in a personal way, but to set an example for others to follow. You have an opportunity to develop the true wisdom that comes from worldly experience and maturity.

What you have already learned

- *To have a purpose*
- *The difference between youth and maturity*
- *To be philosophical*
- *Why it's important to have a goal*
- *A certain amount of wisdom*
- *To see the big picture*
- *To have faith in yourself*
- *That one can't ignore one's responsibilities*

ELEMENTS OF CHARACTER

Your special place in the zodiac

The tenth sign

Capricorn is the tenth sign of the zodiac. Your sign is naturally positioned at the Midheaven, which symbolises the pinnacle of human achievement, the highest point we can reach.

You undertake tasks involving enormous effort because you understand that doing so will pay off in the long run.

This is the zone of sky above our heads, associated with the midday sun, but the Sun moves into Capricorn at the winter solstice, so you appreciate the cycle of the seasons over time. Summer will eventually return, as will winter, so you always conserve your resources and make good use of what is available.

You accept that in order to reap, you must sow. You have no qualms about undertaking tasks involving enormous effort because you understand that doing so will pay off in the long run.

Cardinal earth

Capricorn is a cardinal sign, which means you are a born leader. Of all the cardinal signs—Aries, Cancer, Libra and Capricorn—you are the most adept leader of all, because you are also patient and practical.

The mix of cardinal energy and the earth element makes you like a mountain. Goats like to climb mountains. The top of the mountain is your domain and the view is awe-inspiring.

Because you have such a high vantage point, your perspective is broad. You understand that everything in the world has a specific function and purpose. You are keen to use your resources to build the systems and structures of the world.

YOUR GODS AND MYTHS

Capricorns are pragmatic. You don't really have time for myths and fairytales because there's important work to do.

You always put duty before pleasure. This could have something to do with your last sojourn in Sagittarius, where you had all the fun you could handle.

You always put duty before pleasure. This could have something to do with your last incarnation in Sagittarius, where you had all the fun you could handle.

Being a Capricorn means you're a realist. Your sign is ruled by the planet Saturn.

Saturn—Lord of time

Before the Olympian gods came to power, Saturn/Cronus was in charge. He was a Titan and the lord of time.

Saturn/Cronus was the youngest son of Uranus and Gaia (Earth). Because Uranus feared his children would depose him, he hid them away in the bowels of the Earth. This caused Gaia a great deal of pain, so she came up with a scheme to overthrow her husband and ensure he wouldn't father any more children.

Encouraged by his mother, Cronus castrated his father and threw his genitals into the sea.

He then married his sister Rhea and they had six children: Hestia, Demeter, Hera, Hades, Poseidon and Zeus.[1]

Fearful his children would overthrow him, just as he had deposed his own father, Cronus swallowed each of his children at birth. Rhea saved Zeus by giving her husband a stone to swallow instead.

After Zeus had grown, he compelled his father to regurgitate the five children he had swallowed and led a revolt against his father and the other Titans. Cronus was defeated and Zeus became the supreme god.

At times you feel obliged to play a fatherly role, which is why shouldering responsibilities comes naturally to you, but there's another ancient god you identify with, and he is not quite so saturnine.

Pan—God of the mountainside

Pan was the mischievous god of goats and sheep. He was a satyr, with the horns and hindquarters of a goat. Pan spent most of his time drinking, dancing and chasing nymphs through the forest. He loved music and delighted in playing his panpipes. Like Pan, many Capricorns have musical talent.

Pan loved to play pranks on passers-by, inducing in them a state of 'panic' which is the origin of this word.

Unfortunately, when the church was trying to convert people to Christianity, pagan worship was outlawed and Pan was made a scapegoat.[2]

Pan represents your rustic nature and deep connection with planet Earth.

Though Pan was a trickster, self-indulgent, highly sexed and even rather cranky at times, he wasn't evil or demonic. Pan represents your rustic nature and deep connection with planet Earth, but because Pan has been demonised, you often try to overcome what comes naturally to you.

Consequently, you might feel as if you must rise above nature and strive to be a pillar of respectability.

Pan and Zeus were childhood friends. Pan helped Zeus in his battle with the monstrous Typhon. During the battle, Pan plunged into a river and tried to turn into a fish to escape, but he only managed to transform his lower half, becoming a fish-tailed goat.

Zeus was dismembered by the monster and Pan helped put him back together. As a reward for his assistance, Zeus placed Pan amongst the stars in the constellation Capricorn.[3]

Though at times you might feel like a scapegoat, there's an impish Pan inside you, who loves nothing more than to frolic in the forest.

WHAT YOUR PLANETS REVEAL ABOUT YOU

As far as the ancients knew, Saturn was positioned at the outer edge of our solar system and so Saturn represents limitations and boundaries; in turn, you have a clear understanding of form and structure.

But since the discovery of Uranus in 1781, nothing has been the same. The world was turned upside-down. We now know the universe is infinite and the discoveries keep coming, as do advances in science and technology.

Saturn takes 29 years to orbit the Sun and move through the zodiac. When it completes one full cycle and returns to the position it occupied at birth, we experience what is known astrologically as a 'Saturn return'. The Saturn cycle is one of the most significant planetary cycles.

SECRETS OF THE ZODIAC

The first Saturn return at the age of 29 is associated with maturity, when we must face our adult responsibilities. It is often accompanied by major life events and decisions. We set goals, we marry, we have children, we start our own business, or maybe we change careers, and sometimes fate conspires against us, altering the course of our life. We may run into obstacles preventing us from doing what we want to do. In one way or another we must face our limitations. We also start to realise it's going to take more time to reach our goals than we perhaps thought. Are we prepared to put in the effort? Because Saturn is your ruling planet, when the Saturn return rolls around you are more prepared than most.

At the age of 58, at the next Saturn return, we begin to think about retirement and the next chapter of life. It's between the ages of 29 and 58 when our most important achievements are reached.

New information changes the status quo, and that means new rules come into play. It's not always easy for you to keep up. The rapid pace of change can be an issue for you. You prefer the reliability of order and routine, for this gives you a sense of security.

Saturn represents limitations and boundaries, so you have a clear understanding of form and structure.

As a Capricorn you're in tune with the Saturn cycle. What is the plan forward? Have I achieved what I set out to do? Where to from here? What do I want to achieve in the long-term? These questions are often at the forefront of your mind.

As the saying goes, life was not meant to be easy, but with Saturn as your ruling planet, you accept this, and this gives you a big head start.

WHAT MAKES YOU TICK?

Chances are you were a serious child who enjoyed doing chores and taking on responsibilities. In your spare time maybe you liked playing with building blocks or Lego, constructing houses, roads and miniature infrastructure.

As a child you respected your elders and you still do.

Capricorns are diligent students and favourite subjects include maths, music and history. Before other kids your age you were probably giving serious thought to your career path. You listened to the advice of your parents and teachers, especially when it came to vocational guidance. Maybe you were expected to follow in your father's or mother's footsteps, or were groomed to go into the family business. As a child you respected your elders and you still do.

CAPRICORN

You know that anything worth doing is worth doing well. To achieve success one must be dedicated, thorough and, most of all, disciplined.

A Capricorn friend of mine told me how when she was in primary school she declined an invitation to a classmate's birthday party because she wanted to visit her elderly aunt. This preference for duty is quite natural. You want to do the right thing and be respected. It's important you are seen as a person who has integrity, but that's not the only reason.

You actually enjoy the company of older people. You want to be wiser, and you know your elders have something to teach you. Capricorn children are often wise beyond their years.

You know that anything worth doing is worth doing well. To achieve success, one must be dedicated, thorough and, most of all, disciplined. What is the point if one is not going to apply oneself wholeheartedly? You're incredibly conscientious and always adhere to the codes of society.

As far as you're concerned, everyone should be economical, an upstanding member of the community and work hard.

Unfortunately, there aren't many people who are as conscientious as you, and as far as you're concerned that's the main problem with the world.

You have stamina and endurance and you're prepared to do whatever it takes to climb to the top, and you take great pains to conduct yourself in an ethical manner. There is a right way to do things and a wrong way; that's another important rule.

Regardless of your specific set of rules, you feel duty bound to instil your code of conduct upon others and the world as a whole. As far as you are concerned, everyone should have the same high level of self-discipline as you do. Unfortunately, there aren't many people who are as conscientious as you, and as far as you're concerned that's the main problem with the world.

Because you have such a serious nature, you can be sometimes prone to bouts of depression, but when you are feeling down, try to acknowledge your inner Pan; he will lift your spirits.

In fact there's a prankish trickster lurking within every goat.

While at first glance you appear to be as sure-footed as a mountain goat, only interested in climbing towards worldly success, there's a part of you that's a fish-tailed goat and this part of you is more sensitive, creative, dreamy and emotional.

Yes, you have feelings, but rarely, if ever, do you show them. You play your cards very close to your chest. So close, in fact, that people can find you very difficult to get to know.

You hide your sensitivity beneath a cool and capable exterior, yet deep down there's a soft heart beating in time with the natural rhythms of planet Earth.

Often you are so busy being dutiful that you are not even aware you have needs of your own.

You're not a machine, but flesh and blood. You need to enjoy life more and not take everything so seriously. Pan can help you do this.

One of your most important life lessons is to recognise that you are always free to choose your route to the top of the mountain, and you can always stop before you get there, or take time out to go fishing instead. This doesn't mean you have failed. Maybe you just set your sights too high in the first place?

Once you take a fresh look at the terrain, you'll be amazed at the alternatives available to you. You don't always have to do what you think is expected of you. Now and then why not take the road less travelled and see where it leads?

> *There's a free spirit inside you just waiting to be released.*

Many Capricorns dream of moving out of the big city and living a rural lifestyle, but to take a leap into the unknown you might have to change some of your self-imposed rules, and that can be difficult to do. Like all earth signs, change is not something you handle very well.

You calculate the odds and plan your moves carefully, which is admirable, but perhaps now and then you should take more risks.

Basically, you're a conservative individual. 'Conservative' is generally understood to mean straight-laced and right-wing and maybe you are someone who wears a business suit on the weekend, but most Capricorns are more interested in conservation than in being conservative.

> *Later in life you are likely to kick up your heels and become more capricious, which is another side of your personality.*

Whether you are a greenie, or have a green thumb, being close to nature always lifts your spirits.

In his youth, a Capricorn friend of mine lived for many years in an alternative self-sustaining community. This might seem out of character for a Capricorn, but this was his way of mastering the material world and being conservative. Now retired after a long and successful career, he's a passionate gardener. He grows all his own vegetables organically, composts everything and his garden is filled with native plants. He takes great care to ensure he treads lightly on planet Earth. He has been a committed environmentalist all his life, long before it was fashionable, or necessary.

It's often said Capricorns are old souls who start out in life with a mature head on their strong shoulders, but as the years advance they become more youthful. It's true. Later in life you're more likely to kick up your heels and become more capricious, which is another side of your personality. As you grow older you will probably become more rebellious and eccentric, for you are gradually moving towards the next sign, Aquarius, which is a sign known for its individuality and love of freedom.

Capricorn Sir Isaac Newton was a mathematician, astronomer, physicist, alchemist and philosopher. Over the course of his life he undertook an incredible amount of work and made numerous significant contributions to science. Though best known as a man of science, he was also a spiritual man, who lived a simple life and devoted himself to the study of alchemy in his last years. Newton's third law of motion, for every action there is an equal and opposite reaction, is similar to the metaphysical law of cause and effect, or the concept of karma.

You have a great deal of wisdom. You can become wiser still by keeping your mind open to fresh alternatives. Remember that no matter how industrious you are, you can't possibly reach the summit of every peak.

There's a free spirit inside you just waiting to be released. To really experience what it's like to be wild and free, you just have to change yourself into that strange and rare creature—the goat-fish—and take the plunge.

THE REALLY IMPORTANT THINGS IN YOUR LIFE

Your career and goals

Because you apply yourself to mastering everything you undertake, you can attain success in just about any field. You don't mind how long it takes.

It might take you years to reach the top, but you just put one foot after the other and climb. Your sign is without doubt the most ambitious sign of the zodiac, but you don't go around shouting it out from the mountaintop.

Retirement is probably not part of your long-term plan.
For as long as you are able, you want to be useful.

Working for yourself is appealing and you have the necessary know-how to make it happen.

One day you might be recognised as an authority in your chosen field. Capricorn sportsmen like Muhammad Ali, Tiger Woods and Michael Schumacher, or scientists like Sir Isaac Newton, Louis Pasteur and Stephen Hawking, are some of your role models.

Politics, banking, engineering, public service, town planning or architecture are fields in which you might excel.

If you decide to live in the country, you could make a real go of life as a farmer, primary producer or winemaker.

Music is a more creative field where you might excel, but first and foremost you are practical. If you can't earn a decent living from it, then it will just be a hobby.

Your sign is highly skilled at managing money. Whether or not this makes you materialistic probably depends on each Capricorn's level of soul development and overall attitude. It's not so much money for its own sake that interests you, but what you can achieve with money well spent.

You appreciate quality, but you're also keen on looking for a bargain for you prefer to live within your means. It's equally important to have money put aside just in case you need it.

Capricorns are known to make wise investments and many like to collect antiques. Your love of history and appreciation of time and effort makes you good at spotting the real thing from the copy or reproduction.

Your personal ambitions always have a bigger purpose, for it is civilisation as a whole that you want to build and influence. Ultimately, you want to make the world a better place.

Whatever you undertake you soon ascertain whether or not there's opportunity for advancement, and if not you'll choose another route to the summit.

One day you might be recognised as an authority in your chosen field.

Whether in politics, business, or any other field of endeavour, you set an example to others by showing them how to be responsible and self-disciplined.

But it's important to recognise you have physical limitations. Though you understand limitations and boundaries are essential in life, often you push yourself to the absolute limits of physical endurance.

Health problems associated with Capricorn are mostly connected with overwork. You may be prone to arthritis or other joint or skeletal problems. Other areas to watch are your teeth and your knees. You need to make an effort to look after yourself and not neglect your personal and emotional needs.

Retirement is probably not part of your long-term plan. For as long as you are able, you want to be useful. Later in life you'll have more time on your hands for bushwalking, growing vegetables or playing golf, and maybe even indulging your hidden talents, but always your focus is on doing and keeping busy. You never rest on your laurels.

SHARING YOUR KNOWLEDGE

How you get along with others

People you can teach:	Fire signs—Aries, Leo, Sagittarius
Compatible similar signs:	Earth signs—Taurus, Virgo, Capricorn
Compatible complementary signs:	Water signs—Cancer, Scorpio, Pisces
People you can learn from:	Air signs—Gemini, Libra, Aquarius

Relating to fire signs (Aries, Leo, Sagittarius)

You want to set a good example to others by leading the way. Mostly, you are keen to show the fire signs what to do, for these are the people who have the most trouble managing the material world and who lack self-discipline.

You want them to be more organised and responsible, but annoyingly they're not interested. The more you try to guide them in the right direction, the more they will resist your efforts. Fire signs don't operate according to rules and regulations; they are free spirits, spontaneous and impulsive. They feel restricted and penned in by your efforts to have them see sense.

Regardless of the resistance you encounter, you will keep trying to show them how they can build something lasting with their creative talents.

Fire/Earth relationships tend to be challenging, but you are often attracted to fire signs. They remind you that deep down you are highly creative too. They make you feel carefree and young at heart.

Relating to earth signs (Taurus, Virgo, Capricorn)

Thanks to the stable energy of the earth element, you have incredible staying power. You're amazingly dedicated and reliable. Like your earth sign cousins, Taurus and Virgo, the earth element gives you an ample helping of common sense.

Your relationships with these people are mutually supportive and harmonious, but it's worth mentioning that you can potentially lock horns with other goats. When this happens you might find yourself in a real battle. Who can climb higher? Who is more successful? Who is more ethical? Whose rules are more valid? Who is stronger? This can go on for a long time as you both want to be the boss, but there can only be one winner.

Virgos are a great match for you, especially in any professional or business arrangement.

You have most in common with Virgos; for both of you, duty comes first. Virgos are a great match for you, especially in any professional or business arrangement. You're compatible with Taureans too, but to truly open your heart you would do better with a water sign.

Relating to water signs (Cancer, Scorpio, Pisces)

Potentially, relationships with the water signs are the most supportive relationships you will encounter. They express their emotions and help you do likewise. They also help you acknowledge that you have personal needs of your own. These compassionate people can provide you with emotional support, and you can provide them with the security they seek.

When you are around water signs you are somehow more relaxed. You are especially compatible with Pisceans. They help to bring out your creative and softer side, your Pan nature.

When you are around water signs you are somehow more relaxed.

You're compatible with Scorpios too, though you both have a need to be in charge, which can sometimes lead to conflict and competition.

Cancer is your opposite sign, so there is often a magnetic fascination that draws you towards these sensitive lunar types. But in relationships with Cancerians you can end up playing the role of parent to their child.

Relating to air signs (Gemini, Libra, Aquarius)

People born under the air signs can teach you some important life lessons, but these are the very people you find most frustrating.

As far as you're concerned, there are ways to do things and ways not to do things, but air signs have a completely different approach. This makes it virtually impossible for you to exert your influence over them.

Air signs really get on your goat, but they can teach you a lot of new things.

WHAT YOU NEED TO LEARN

To think outside the square

You want more than anything to improve the world and have others do likewise, but you are in danger of becoming overly strict and rigid. You need to realise that you cannot force square pegs into round holes. Deep down you are not such a square peg either; you have soft round curves to your personality—that watery tail that you often pretend doesn't exist.

The more others want to change the status quo, the more you try to enforce your rules. You need to learn that not everyone sees things the way you do. Beyond your boundaries and parameters, there are new frontiers just waiting to be discovered.

You cannot force square pegs into round holes.

Accept it, each person is unique. You might have grand plans and ambitions and even want to make the world a better place, but other people have different goals and aims. You need to take into account these individual differences.

*History teaches us important lessons, and you are the
first to take history into account when formulating your
rules and systems, but what about the future?*

People are not cardboard cut-outs. They're human, as are you. Everyone is different. Each person has their own set of rules, and some people have no rules at all!

Sometimes you can be so focused on your personal ambitions you fail to see the wider social implications of your actions and how they affect the community as a whole.

History teaches us important lessons, and you are the first to take history into account when formulating your rules and systems, but what about the future? If you continually stick to the rules, you run the risk of being stuck in a time warp, and even you can't stop time from moving forward.

As new information, fresh ideas and new discoveries are made, you can get left behind, but the air signs can show you the way forward and how to think outside the square.

TAKING THE NEXT STEP

The air signs—Gemini, Libra and Aquarius—can introduce you to technology, help you cope with change and show you how to adapt to the future as it unfolds.

Air signs are good communicators and highly social. They can teach you how to communicate more effectively and, most importantly, show you there are broader implications to your systems and goals.

But as a rule, you find air signs rather frivolous and superficial. They don't seem to take things seriously.

Geminis are the chatterboxes of the zodiac. You see them as totally unreliable because they never sit still for a second and they are constantly changing their tune from one moment to the next. But Geminis can show you how to cope with changing circumstances and how to be more adaptable.

Librans have leadership skills like you, but they seem to go about it in a most peculiar way. They actually consult with others first. They take into account the differences between people. They can teach you how to cooperate with others.

Aquarians confound you more than any other sign. Yet you have something in common with Aquarians, for although they are ruled by the rebel planet Uranus, they are co-ruled by Saturn, the same planet you know so much about.

You can be reluctant to try new approaches, for the tried and tested methods take precedence.

Aquarians can show you how to walk on the wild side and you do have a wild side, care of Pan's influence; it's just that Saturn constantly seems to tell you to be responsible and self-disciplined.

You can be reluctant to try new approaches, for the tried and tested methods take precedence, but Aquarians can show you how to keep an open mind and think differently.

Sometimes you can be a tad anti-social too. You prefer to live within the confines of Saturn, with its rings, boundaries and structures, even if this isolates you from people. Uranus is a whole new frontier, full of innovative ideas and interesting people, but you feel decidedly uncomfortable when everything is turned upside-down and sideways. Nothing and no one can be relied upon to function the way it should! It unsettles you no end.

But in the midst of this chaos and free-thinking comes the genesis of new ideas, inventions and discoveries which are the real foundation of civilisation.

If you listen to what the air signs are saying, you'll soon see there is merit in their thinking. Aquarians especially have an instinct for what the future holds, and so they can take your plans and systems and bring them up-to-date so they will last well into the future.

You need to understand that rules must be modified to take into account individual differences and allow for progress.

If you let the air signs teach you, they can show you how to cope with change and how to open your mind to fresh ways of seeing the world. Don't worry; the world will not suddenly come to an end if you don't always put duty first.

This can give you a real sense of freedom that you never knew before.

TIPS FOR CAPRICORN

♑ Recognise you have needs like everyone else.
♑ Once in a while delegate some of your responsibilities.
♑ Be open to new ideas and different viewpoints.
♑ Now and then take a detour just to see where it leads.
♑ Recognise that others may have more knowledge than you.
♑ Occasionally do something spontaneous and creative just for fun.
♑ Consider the advice of the air signs you meet.

YOUR GIFT TO THE WORLD

How you can make a real difference

Your special gift to the world is your sure-footedness. Whatever the terrain, you know how to overcome the challenge and climb to the summit. If everyone on Earth were a Capricorn, we would all take personal responsibility and strive to make the world a better place.

Though you struggle to think outside the square at times, your professional approach to everything you do is to be commended. You set a fine example. People can learn from you that through hard work one can achieve respect and rise to the top. When you are feeling melancholy, remind yourself you are only human and are doing the very best you can. And don't forget to take time out now and then to frolic in the forest.

FAMOUS PERSONALITIES WITH THE SUN IN CAPRICORN INCLUDE:

Muhammad Ali
Shirley Bassey
David Bowie
Bob Brown
Nicholas Cage
Jim Carrey
Joan of Arc
Marlene Dietrich
Dian Fossey
Cary Grant
Stephen Hawking
J. Edgar Hoover

Anthony Hopkins
Howard Hughes
Paul Keating
Martin Luther King, Jr
Isaac Newton
Richard Nixon
Louis Pasteur
Elvis Presley
Michael Schumacher
Albert Schweitzer
Joseph Stalin
Tiger Woods

AQUARIUS

21 JANUARY–19 FEBRUARY

'Hell, there are no rules here, we are trying to
accomplish something.'

AQUARIUS, THOMAS EDISON

YOUR LIFE MISSION

To know the truth. To use this knowledge to improve individual freedoms for the future progress of humanity.

As an Aquarian you are a bit of a square peg. You're interested in everything from complex social issues and the latest technology, to what your neighbours had for breakfast last Wednesday.

But in fact you're not really worried about the neighbours' breakfast; it's just that having this information helps you formulate your ideas and theories about how the world and society works, and that does matter.

The individual doesn't really interest you as much as the whole group, but at the same time being free to express your unique individuality is essential. You want to stand apart from the group and go your own way and do all you can to help others do likewise.

There are a number of apparent contradictions at the heart of your sign and for this reason others often misunderstand you. For one thing, Aquarius is an air sign, not a water sign, as many people think.

You're interested in everything from complex social issues and the latest technology, to what your neighbours had for breakfast last Wednesday.

Although you are a true humanitarian and really care about the plight of humanity, at times you can lack real compassion because you go about your mission like a scientist conducting an experiment.

What you really want to get at is the truth, the whole truth and nothing but the truth, so help you God.

God? Yes, I know, you're probably an atheist, most Aquarians are. You're highly sceptical about anything to do with religion and faith, and given the misery inflicted upon the human race in the name of religion, who can blame you? But this issue goes to the core of your dilemma.

As far as you are concerned, anything you cannot explain rationally is complete hogwash, and blind faith definitely comes under this heading.

What you really want to get at is the truth, the whole truth and nothing but the truth.

You're clever and you know it, and everyone else knows it too. So if you can't explain it, it must be rubbish, right? Well, maybe.

You want very much to discover the truth, so you're always asking really difficult questions. Throughout the ages the best minds, many of them Aquarian, have sought the truth.

The fact remains that your insatiable quest for a rational explanation to life and its many mysteries keeps bringing you face-to-face with questions of faith and belief.

There are a number of apparent contradictions at the heart of your sign so people often misunderstand you. For one thing, Aquarius is an air sign, not a water sign, as many people think.

What's the meaning of life? How can human suffering be explained? What happens after we die? What is the truth about faith? How did the universe come into being? These questions always lead you towards the mystical, the esoteric and the spiritual, and that's when you start to feel uncomfortable. Some things always seem to elude you, and that's because not everything can be explained scientifically.

So if you remain sceptical, objective, rational and detached, how can you hope to answer these questions? How can you ever know the ultimate truth?

GIFTS FROM THE PAST

We're almost at the end of the zodiac. Aquarius is the third air sign so you have accumulated a fair amount of life experience. The last three signs have a truly universal outlook.

Capricorn taught you to be self-disciplined and realistic. You understand the world and its systems, but now you are keen to ensure that they stand the test of time well into the future—if they don't, it is up to you to bring about reform.

What you have already learned

- *All about systems and procedures*
- *To be pragmatic and realistic*
- *To achieve something significant one needs to work hard*
- *To understand the way the world is organised and structured*
- *To be self-disciplined*
- *To live life according to your core principles*
- *That rules sometimes need to be altered for progress to happen*

ELEMENTS OF CHARACTER

Your special place in the zodiac

The eleventh sign

Aquarius is the eleventh sign of the zodiac. At Capricorn we reach a pinnacle of achievement, but now you are asking yourself what lies beyond these achievements. Where are things headed? What are these achievements really for? You want to know all there is to know and to share your knowledge for the future betterment of humanity.

Fixed air

When I was first learning astrology I couldn't quite get my head around how air could be fixed. It seems like a contradiction. You too can be a bit of a contradiction.

You can blow hot and cold, but, like the wind,
you like to be free.

All over the globe there are prevailing winds. It might be a hot nor-wester, a howling southerly buster, a ferocious hurricane, or a gentle afternoon sea breeze. But even when there is no wind at all, we know it will come back in one form or another, for there is a pattern to it, even though that pattern is not always regular.

The wind is free to blow in a variety of ways and it's just the same with you. You can blow hot and cold, but, like the wind, you like to be free.

Atmospheric currents drive our weather systems, but the weather is always changing, especially these days. Chances are it will be an Aquarian who comes up with the solution to the problem of climate change.

Chances are it will be an Aquarian who comes up with
the solution to the problem of climate change.

The mix of fixed energy with the air element gives you fantastic powers of concentration. You are always thinking ahead, and developing new theories and ideas.

The Sun is in Aquarius in midwinter. This is the coldest time of the year, the hottest in the southern hemisphere. These extremes of temperature are characteristic of your sign, which is known to go to extremes.

February is a month of snow, ice and rain, when water from the heavens nourishes the Earth. The word 'February' means 'to purify' or 'to cleanse'.

Another reason people think Aquarius is a water sign is because 'aqua' means water, adding to the confusion.

YOUR GODS AND MYTHS

The first four signs of the zodiac—Aries, Taurus, Gemini and Cancer—are associated with what we might call the preschool of our personal development, where first and foremost, we are learning about ourselves.

The middle four signs—Leo Virgo, Libra and Scorpio—are associated with adult maturity, where we learn to express ourselves, develop more self-awareness and learn to relate to others.

The last four signs—Sagittarius, Capricorn, Aquarius and Pisces—are more universal in outlook and interested in the big picture. Your focus is on the individual's relationship to the world, society and beyond. You are broadminded and a real humanitarian.

Uranus—The original sky god

According to the Greek creation story, Gaia (Earth) emerged from primordial Chaos and gave birth to Uranus. Uranus and Gaia married and Uranus fathered the Titans, including Saturn/Cronus, who in turn fathered the Olympian gods.

Uranus was fearful his children would depose him so he confined his offspring in the bowels of the Earth.

This caused Gaia a great deal of pain. She encouraged her son Saturn to castrate Uranus so he could not have any more children. Saturn used a sickle for the deed, tossing his father's genitals into the sea. From this act was born the beautiful Venus/Aphrodite, the goddess of love.

Creative freedom was important to Uranus and it is important to you too. Just as he was the original sky god, you too are an original.

You want to create the future as you see fit and you like to have things your own way. It's important to keep in mind that the freedom to do as you please is not your freedom exclusively.

The whole pantheon of gods came into being as a result of Uranus being overthrown.

Though you perhaps fear what might happen in a future where you have no power to determine events, deep down you also know that the freedom to create is a universal desire shared by all living things.

Saturn—Lord of time

Since the discovery of Uranus in 1781, many astrologers have assigned Uranus as your ruling planet, but for thousands of years before this, Saturn was your traditional ruling planet.[1]

Having two ruling planets is in keeping with the nature of Aquarius, for your sign is a sign of duality, as symbolised by your glyph ♒.

Basically, there are two types of Aquarians, those whose personalities are more in keeping with Saturn and those who are more like Uranus. If you are one of the Saturn types, you are probably more like a Capricorn. The key difference is that Saturn types do things by the book and live in the reality of here and now, while the Uranus types are less interested in conventions and more interested in the future.

Basically there are two types of Aquarians, those whose personalities are more in keeping with Saturn and those who are more like Uranus.

Aquarian men and women are often quite different from one another too; the women on the whole are more grounded and earthy than the men and tend to have more in common with the typical Capricorn.

Ganymede—The cup bearer

Another mythic character associated with Aquarius is Ganymede, who was a handsome Trojan prince. Jupiter/Zeus fell in love with the youth and abducted him, taking him to Olympus to be his lover.

Zeus decided to make Ganymede his cup-bearer. It was Ganymede's job to pour ambrosia, the nectar of the gods. This was the elixir of life, the source of immortality. Zeus honoured Ganymede by placing him among the stars in the constellation Aquarius.[2]

Jupiter's largest Moon is named after Ganymede. It's the largest satellite in the solar system, bigger even than Mercury.

Just as Ganymede poured the elixir of life, you are also a vessel from which knowledge is poured forth.

Ganymede is associated with homosexual love. Regardless of your sexual orientation, Aquarians often have a unisex way of thinking. Just as in other areas of your life, when it comes to sex you can be difficult to categorise. Some Aquarians are quite asexual, some bisexual, while others are open to sexual experimentation and the idea of open marriage can appeal.

Prometheus—Rebellious god of foresight

Prometheus is another god associated with your sign. He was a grandson of Uranus.

Prometheus, whose name means foresight, is said to have created the first human from clay and water. He also taught arts and sciences, including astronomy, to the human race.

Jupiter/Zeus was furious that his authority was being undermined in this way and withheld fire from humans who were forced to live in the cold and dark. Prometheus decided to steal fire from the gods and give it to the people too.

Enraged, Zeus sent a great flood to destroy the human race, but Prometheus warned the people of the approaching deluge and the people were saved.[3]

Like Prometheus you are a rebel and an outsider.
You have no qualms about breaking with tradition or
standing up to authority.

Zeus chained Prometheus to a rock as punishment and sent an eagle to peck at his liver, but it kept growing back. His torture is said to have lasted thousands of years until he was eventually set free.

Like Prometheus you are a rebel and an outsider and like to raise consciousness in others. You have no qualms about breaking with tradition or standing up to authority in order to do this.

WHAT YOUR PLANETS REVEAL ABOUT YOU

Uranus is an odd planet, it doesn't conform, and nor do you. Unlike all the other planets, Uranus rotates on an axis of around 90 degrees, rolling through space like a huge aqua-coloured beach ball. It also has a strange magnetic field like a giant corkscrew.

Uranus orbits the Sun in 84 years, which corresponds closely to one human lifetime. Similarly, Uranus can almost be seen with the naked eye; it therefore symbolises the limits of human conscious awareness.

If we divide the Uranus orbit of 84 years into equal quadrants, we have the four main stages of human development.

Uranus was discovered in 1781, midway between the French and American revolutions, a time of dramatic upheaval. 'Liberty, equality and fraternity' was the catchcry of the day. People were rebelling against authority and were seeking freedom and democracy. The Industrial Revolution was also ushering in tremendous social changes as new inventions and discoveries came in rapid succession.

Uranus is an odd planet, it doesn't conform, and nor do you.

At the age of 21 we arrive into independent adulthood. Then at 42 we reach midlife, which is often a time of rebellion, creativity and change. By this time we have generally developed a fair amount of self-knowledge. At 63 we experience another important change, as we leave our most productive years behind us and begin a new chapter of contemplation and freedom. With any luck by 84 we've obtained some wisdom.

You may have noticed that major life events, changes and decisions happen every seven years.

While individual circumstances will of course vary, these stages of life are true for all of us, but as Uranus is your ruling planet, you are perhaps more in tune with this cycle.

You may have noticed that major life events, changes and decisions happen every seven years. This is due to the fact that the Uranus and Saturn[4] cycles are linked. There are four seven-year periods in one Saturn cycle and twelve seven-year periods in a Uranus cycle. Uranus spends seven years in each sign of the zodiac.

WHAT MAKES YOU TICK?

When you were a child you were probably one of those kids who enjoyed dissecting insects. Maybe you liked to experiment with your chemistry set and once blew up your cubby house, or dyed the neighbour's cat blue, just to see what would happen.

Aquarian children are highly intelligent, curious about everything and like to work things out for themselves. It probably only took you a nanosecond to solve the Rubik's Cube. Perhaps you were a child prodigy, many Aquarian children are.

Because you have an exceptional mind, capable of both flashes of insight and deep analysis, you can be frustrated by the comparatively slow pace of academic learning. You can quickly become bored.

With the possible exception of the odd Virgo, no other sign can analyse as quickly as you. But unlike Virgo, you see not only the immediate problem and its solution, but the broader implications for society, and how your solution can be adapted to meet future needs.

Perhaps you were a child prodigy, many Aquarian children are.

Ninety-nine per cent of the time you live in your head. You're an idealist to the core and have an iron-clad set of principles by which you live your life, and to which you think the world should adhere. These principles include knowledge, freedom, independence, social justice and truth, and are all incredibly important to you.

You like to remain objective and impartial so you tend to approach relationships this way too, which can make you seem rather aloof and distant, which is a pity because you are a great friend and your friends are very important to you.

Sometimes you can be so focused on your theories and principles you can hurt others' feelings without meaning to.

All air signs are sociable and love company, but you are not as sociable as either Gemini or Libra because there are times when you need your own space too. Like Virgos and Cancerians, you need time alone now and then, but your desire for solitude is usually only short-lived. You have an equal need to be part of the community, yet also need the freedom to go your own way.

You're an idealist to the core and have an iron-clad set of principles by which you live your life.

These inconsistencies are just a few of your personality quirks. Like your ruling planet Uranus, you can be quite erratic at times; but being a

fixed air sign, when you hit upon an idea that interests you, there's no stopping you.

Just when people have made up their minds that you are anti-social, completely weird or disinterested, suddenly you come up with the exact observation or gesture that changes their opinion.

There's a bit of the 'mad scientist' about you. You enjoy having the most up-to-date gadgets and delight in figuring out how they work, but like Sagittarians, your curiosity can sometimes lead to mishaps.

Many years ago I worked for an Aquarian boss. One day he was walking back to his office from the photocopy room, looking quite dishevelled and in an obvious state of shock. We all took one look at him and burst out laughing. Curious to know how the new paper-shredder worked, he had leant forward for a closer inspection and whoosh! It had gobbled up his tie. In a flash he hit the stop button and managed to disentangle himself. He was quite lucky really, for he might easily have caused himself a serious injury, but he looked so funny that the whole office was in hysterics for months. Anyway, he found out how the shredder worked.

Aquarians are light years ahead of their time.
The only drawback to being so clever is that it makes
you an outsider.

Aquarians are not usually comfortable in positions of authority, yet many take on leadership roles. A career in politics might appeal; indeed any occupation that provides scope for social improvement and progress. You're equally suited to jobs where technology plays a part. There are lots of options available, so long as you don't get bored. Computer programmer is an obvious choice. Other options include the social sciences, research, electrical engineering, any of the sciences, chemist, or inventor. Autonomy is important to you, but like Librans you enjoy working in a team environment too.

Sometimes you inadvertently cause problems for your colleagues because they have to stop what they're doing and change tack to accommodate your vision. With your lightning-quick perceptions and ability to think ahead, you have a tendency to jump the gun. You see the future ramifications so clearly you know right away if a particular approach will work in the longer term. But that longer term might be 50 or 100 years from now, and no one but you can see that far ahead.

Like the planet Uranus, you can leave a giant corkscrew of chaos in your wake, but you don't see it that way. You just wish everyone would hurry and catch on and see what you are trying to accomplish.

One of your key interests is to improve the world and ensure that the system actually provides for the whole community. When you see how the establishment is failing, you have no hesitation in doing whatever it takes to bring about reform, for you are driven by a compelling desire to create a better future.

Sometimes you just have to take things on faith.

Some Aquarians are light years ahead of their time.

We all have electricity surging through our brains, but you have unique circuits that make flashes of insight fairly commonplace. The only drawback to being so brilliant is that it can make you a bit of an outsider.

In conversation you use long words when short ones would do. It's not that you're trying to appear clever, for appearances don't interest you in the slightest. This is just the natural way your mind operates. Your brain is highly developed, in fact Aquarius is the sign of true genius, but this usually means the section of your brain where feelings and emotions are housed is under-utilised, which can make you rather absent-minded, insensitive and lacking in compassion.

Yet it's actually this part of the brain which is the gateway to the unconscious, and the source of those amazing flashes of intuition that come to you when you least expect it. You can access this magical realm, it's just that you have trouble understanding how it works and you cannot control it. You want so much to get at the truth, but you tend to undervalue anything you can't fathom intellectually.

It's human nature to become more sensitive and compassionate when we suffer. You can develop more compassion by letting yourself feel emotions rather than trying to examine feelings under a microscope.

As you mature, you're heading towards Pisces. Over time you will begin to see the importance of developing more empathy, but on the whole you prefer to remain impartial, objective and detached.

Aquarian novelist Charles Dickens is best known for his rich characters and tales set amid the suffering and poverty of 19th century London. His novels contain graphic detail about the many social problems and hardships of his day. Dickens started out as a political journalist, becoming an energetic campaigner on behalf of the poor. At around the same time, across the Atlantic, Aquarian Abraham Lincoln was ushering in a period of social reform through the abolition of slavery.

More than anything you want everyone to wake up and become more aware. You want the human race to progress to a higher state of consciousness. But you often fail to realise it's the unconscious which is the source of consciousness.[5] Once you do, this will help you find the answers to life's deepest mysteries.

After the age of 42, you will probably become more interested in developing some kind of belief system. It's then we start to realise we are not immortal.

Everyone goes through a midlife crisis, and for you this can be a crisis of faith.

Try to accept that there are always going to be mysteries, things in life that cannot be explained scientifically. One day perhaps you might discover how and why astrology works, but you'll never know if you don't first believe it's possible.

There are more things under heaven than even you can possibly fathom and perhaps we will never be able to explain them. Sometimes you just have to take things on faith.

THE REALLY IMPORTANT THINGS IN YOUR LIFE

Your friends

Like all air signs you are a people person. Spending time with your friends is one of the most important things in your life. You probably have a wide circle of acquaintances of varied backgrounds, ages and interests.

Sometimes you turn up on Tuesday, when it's actually Friday.

AQUARIUS

Ask ten of your friends for their opinion of you, and you'll get ten different responses. They could be describing different people. There's really no such thing as a typical Aquarian.

Your sign is possibly the most original and quirky sign of the zodiac, which makes you difficult to pigeonhole, and the truth is you really don't like being pigeonholed.

Joining in group activities is vital to your wellbeing; friends make your life worthwhile. You may have several different groups of friends, each having a particular interest or shared activity at its heart.

One Aquarian I know goes to a regular trivia night. The trick to winning at trivia is for each team member to have a specialist area of knowledge. His team includes four Aquarians; one is a maths wiz, one a geography specialist, one is a music guru who is also into sport and pop culture, and another knows everything the others don't. Needless to say they always win.

There's really no such thing as a typical Aquarian.

If a friend suggests sky-diving, or hot-air ballooning, you're the first in line. But it's probably best if you don't offer to make the arrangements as you are not the best organiser in the zodiac, and can be forgetful.

You can easily become sidetracked. Aquarians are always going off on tangents. You just popped in to the cinema to see the latest sci-fi release, or ran into an old friend and had to tell them about the show at the planetarium, and it slipped your mind. Sometimes you turn up on Tuesday, when it's actually Friday.

These kinds of slip-ups happen chiefly because your mind is so crammed full of information that you don't have room for anything else. Though on the one hand Aquarians are the most intelligent beings on the planet, sometimes they give the impression of having no brain at all. You can forget the most obvious things, like your name. There is something of the absent-minded professor about you.

Though on the one hand Aquarians are the most intelligent beings on the planet, sometimes they give the impression of having no brain at all.

On the whole you prefer intellectual companionship to long-term commitment for you easily become bored, which is why Aquarians often hook up with other Aquarians. That way you can keep life interesting and happily avoid anything too emotional or deep.

Aquarian/Aquarian relationships are fairly common because you like the freedom to come and go and you really enjoy each other's company. Many Aquarians opt for unconventional relationships, and may even live in separate houses or in different states or countries. The typical Aquarian is not really interested in the conventions of a committed marriage and children. Many Aquarians choose not to procreate, but prefer to create, invent or discover.

This is partly because you realise there are far too many people living on planet Earth already, a situation which is unsustainable. Because you see the future so clearly, and are committed to your principles, having children is not often on the Aquarian agenda. No one can accuse you of being a hypocrite.

If you do settle down in a committed relationship, it's sure to be unconventional in one way or another. And if it's with another Aquarian at least you know that if you ever go your separate ways, you will always stay friends.

SHARING YOUR KNOWLEDGE

How you get along with others

People you can teach:	Earth signs—Taurus, Virgo, Capricorn
Compatible similar signs:	Air signs—Gemini, Libra, Aquarius
Compatible complementary signs:	Fire signs—Aries, Leo, Sagittarius
People you can learn from:	Water signs—Cancer, Scorpio, Pisces

Relating to earth signs (Taurus, Virgo, Capricorn)

As soon as you come up with a new theory, you particularly enjoy sharing it with the earth signs, for they share and appreciate your rational and logical point of view.

Taureans, Virgos and Capricorns are not very sociable people, but you can see how they could be more useful to the world, if only they would interact more. You want to help them by exposing them to a wider audience.

But earth signs are reluctant to be encouraged in this way. They really don't like being told what to do and will resist your efforts to make them more outgoing and involved. They prefer to go at their own pace which is slower and more measured than yours.

On the whole, relationships between air and earth signs take place in the rational and logical world of the left-brain. You enjoy discussing world events, work or politics, but rarely, if ever, do you talk about emotions, feelings or your inner life.

Relating to air signs (Gemini, Libra, Aquarius)

Most of your friends are probably air signs. All air signs are social creatures who love to communicate.

Because you are not really looking for an emotional connection, you like to relate to other air signs, who are just as interesting as you. As far as you're concerned, friendship is the most important thing anyway.

But there are other people on the planet besides air signs and earth signs and there are times when you will have to relate to some of them too.

Relating to fire signs (Aries, Leo, Sagittarius)

Fire and air are compatible elements. Fire signs are more in touch with their instincts, imagination and the unconscious than you, and can open you up to the magical world of creativity. For this reason they can inspire you like no other people can.

Sagittarius is probably your most compatible sign, for you have a great deal in common and also complement one another. You like Aries people too, for you respect them for their drive and initiative. Leo is your opposite sign so you find Leos incredibly magnetic and fascinating, but after a while you will probably see them as totally self-absorbed. Even so, you can learn a lot from Leos, just as they can from you.

Fire signs can open you up to the magical world of creativity and can inspire you like no other people can.

Relating to water signs (Cancer, Scorpio, Pisces)

It's one of the many curious quirks of your sign that it has so much watery symbolism. This suggests that although you are an air sign, you can potentially also learn to become more compassionate, imaginative and spiritual.

Water signs can help bring real depth and meaning to your life; and this is actually what you most need. By interacting with water signs you will evolve. Water signs know all about the unconscious depths of the psyche; in this they know far more than you.

WHAT YOU NEED TO LEARN

To believe in miracles

Why do people fall for all this pseudo-spiritual mumbo-jumbo? People can be so incredibly gullible. They should be free and independent thinkers and rely solely on their powers of intellect and reasoning. Or so you think.

You have evolved to the highest intellectual level, but this doesn't mean you know everything. There are a host of mysteries you know nothing about. These mysteries reside in the unconscious and it's the water signs that have the most access to this domain.

The unconscious mind operates according to beliefs, emotions and the imagination. It's irrational, which is why you find it so incomprehensible. You think that a coincidence is just coincidence, it doesn't mean anything, but as water signs will tell you, if it feels meaningful, then it is. Whether or not you can explain it scientifically or rationally is irrelevant.

Have you ever heard of the placebo effect? It's not the substance that heals; it's the belief itself that heals. Belief is a powerful drug. It's the power of the unconscious that works this magic. It's the same reason hypnosis and meditation work, but as far as you are concerned many of these topics fall under the heading of complete nonsense. You are automatically sceptical about anything that bypasses your rational thought processes. But at the end of the day, what does it matter?

It's the same thing when life imitates art, or when you have a premonition, or a flash of insight that turns out to be exactly right. Dreams do come true. When you start to believe in miracles you'll see how everything everywhere is magically connected. Then you will truly be free.

TAKING THE NEXT STEP

The more you avoid feeling emotions, the more aloof you become. Your friends, who are so important to you, can begin to see you as cold and distant and start to give you the cold shoulder. This is disturbing and makes you feel bad. See, so you do have feelings after all!

But all feelings aren't bad feelings, there are other emotions too, you just need to open your heart and water signs can help you learn about them.

Cancer, Scorpio and Pisces can teach you to be more compassionate. They want to guide you gently into their world of emotions and teach you something about the spiritual and mystical side of life.

Water signs drive air signs crazy. Though you might be more consciously evolved than water, you fail to see they are imbued with the wisdom of the unconscious, which is infinitely deep.

Just like you want to help the earth signs to be more social and outgoing, the water signs want to help you to understand something about the unconscious.

But on the whole you think water signs are completely irrational, even stupid. What you need to realise is there is also such a thing as emotional intelligence. They have it and you don't.

> *What you need to realise is there is also such a thing as emotional intelligence.*

Cancerians, Scorpios and Pisceans know all about the mysteries of life and seem to have strange magical powers that you find both fascinating and yet impossible to comprehend.

While you are incredibly gifted intellectually, you're really uncomfortable when it comes to matters of the heart.

Because they want you to evolve, water signs are keen to teach you about feelings and the unconscious; but they don't do this by talking to you about it, or by explaining how it works, they communicate in other, more subtle ways. They use imagination and symbolism and inference, even telepathy.

While your conscious mind is highly developed, water signs can introduce you to the magic of the unconscious, which is the source of your knowledge.

Pisces is the sign that follows Aquarius. This enigmatic, spiritual and psychic sign understands the deepest mysteries of life.

Just keep an open mind and you will soon learn to open your heart and spirit too. Though you will never turn into a Piscean, you can access this watery realm—you are an Aqua-rian after all.

TIPS FOR AQUARIUS

- ♒ Try to be a little more compassionate.
- ♒ Don't be afraid of anything you can't explain.
- ♒ Learn to appreciate emotional intelligence as well as intellectual intelligence.
- ♒ Learn to meditate.
- ♒ Realise not everything has a rational explanation.
- ♒ Acknowledge that mystical and spiritual subjects can also be scientific.
- ♒ Consider the advice of the water signs you meet.

YOUR GIFT TO THE WORLD

How you can make a real difference

Your special gift to the world is your inventive mind. Your insight and rapid understanding of often complex ideas is second to none. If the entire human race were Aquarians, no one could use ignorance as an excuse. Everyone would have their consciousness raised to the highest possible level.

Maybe you do need to develop more compassion and deeper spiritual understanding, but your true gift is helping others wake up to themselves and to the amazing possibilities that the future holds.

FAMOUS PERSONALITIES WITH THE SUN IN AQUARIUS INCLUDE:

Alan Alda
Francis Bacon
Alice Cooper
Charles Darwin
James Dean
Charles Dickens
Thomas Edison
Tim Flannery
Germaine Greer
Barry Humphries
James Joyce
Charles Kingsford Smith

Abraham Lincoln
Charles Lindbergh
Norman Mailer
Bob Marley
John McEnroe
Wolfgang Mozart
Rasputin
John Travolta
Jules Verne
Robbie Williams
Oprah Winfrey
Virginia Woolf

PISCES

20 FEBRUARY–20 MARCH

'Imagination is more important than knowledge. For knowledge is limited to all we now know and understand, while imagination embraces the entire world, and all there ever will be to know and understand.'

PISCES, ALBERT EINSTEIN

YOUR LIFE MISSION

To feel you belong to the soul of the universe. To swim in a current of infinite understanding.

Pisces is the twelfth and last sign of the zodiac and therefore contains the accumulated wisdom of the earlier eleven signs. It's as if you have arrived at the end of a very long voyage and now it's time to rest, sleep and dream.

Yet this isn't really the end. That's just an illusion. The zodiac is a spiralling wheel that carries us on an infinite journey.

Just because your sign is considered to be spiritually evolved, this doesn't mean you have nothing more to learn. None of us has reached spiritual perfection, except perhaps a few special souls who have inspired humanity through their teachings and wisdom.

We are all at different stages of spiritual development. There's good and bad in every individual and in every sign of the zodiac, though you prefer to see only the good in people.

You view the world through a truly universal lens. Your consciousness is a cosmic consciousness. Somehow you understand what lies beyond this world and part of you yearns to merge with this divine source of life.

You have buckets of compassion and oceans of understanding.

Maybe you feel you have been here before. It's not uncommon for Pisces people to recall their past lives. Many Pisceans are psychic too. You're a dreamer. Your attention is elsewhere, somewhere beyond the here and now.

It's living in the real world with all its stresses and problems that is your biggest challenge. Basically, you'd rather just go fishing.

You're content to go where the current of life takes you, to just drift with the tide. You're completely selfless and ready to sacrifice your personal needs for the wellbeing of others. You have buckets of compassion and oceans of understanding.

SECRETS OF THE ZODIAC

Your mission is one of the most difficult for others to understand because it isn't really tangible; yours is a mission of the soul.

All living things possess a spiritual life force; a mystical energy that can't really be explained, but can only be felt. You feel this soulful resonance most of the time. When you connect with people, or with animals, or with nature itself, you are uplifted.

Though you would probably prefer to be a monk and live your life in quiet contemplation, there are bigger fish to fry. Your challenge is to fight your way upstream, like salmon returning to their birthplace to spawn. Your hardest task in life is to find the courage, inner strength and initiative to meet the challenges of the real world.

Because Pisces is symbolised by two fish tied together, it can be difficult to know which way is upstream and which is down. Can you go both ways at the same time, or would it be better to just tread water? Some Pisceans find this struggle too overwhelming and end up drowning their troubles in alcohol or drugs.

Substance abuse is an easy trap to fall into, but disillusionment need not lead you on a downward spiral. The type of spiritual experience you are really looking for is not found in a glass at the local pub.

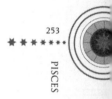

Your mission is one of the most difficult for others to understand because it isn't really tangible. Yours is a mission of the soul.

How and where do you find the strength to fight your way upstream? Why struggle if you always go belly up? What is the point of it all? Who are you really?

You are just so fluid, it's almost like you don't really exist, and yet here you are.

So let's swim in your mysterious currents for a while and see if we can find out who you really are and how you can learn to believe in yourself, just as much as you believe in miracles.

GIFTS FROM THE PAST

It's often said that Pisceans have within them a little bit of every other sign. This is why you are wise. You empathise with everyone. Aquarius taught you to respect humanity as whole. You developed a humanitarian and broadminded view of the world, and a kind of group consciousness. Now you are taking the next step towards truly universal understanding.

Since the universe is a big place, many people are easily overwhelmed by the sheer magnitude of it all, and prefer not to think about the big picture, but your vision and perspective makes you ideally suited to the task.

What you have already learned

- *To see things from a group perspective*
- *To develop your consciousness to a high level*
- *To be concerned about humanity*
- *To glimpse what the future might hold*
- *To comprehend theoretical and scientific principles*
- *To be broadminded*
- *To think outside the square*
- *To trust your intuition*

ELEMENTS OF CHARACTER

Your special place in the zodiac

The twelfth sign

We have walked on the Moon, sent missions to the planets and witnessed vast spiralling galaxies being born in the deepest reaches of space; we have cured diseases and discovered the microcosmic structure of DNA;

but our ocean depths remain a mystery. You too are deep, unfathomable and mysterious.

The natural position of your sign is the twelfth house, which is the 30 degrees of sky just above the horizon, where the Sun, the Moon and planets rise each day, suggesting that your sign is highly visible; but in fact this is just one of many Piscean paradoxes. In one sense your sign is the most aware and enlightened, but you are also deeply mysterious.

As darkness turns to day and day to night, you act as a kind of conduit between the light of consciousness and the mysteries of the unconscious. Potentially, you can illuminate and enlighten the world. More than any other sign, you understand the collective unconscious.

Mutable water

Like Gemini, Virgo and Sagittarius, Pisces is a mutable sign, so you are versatile and adaptable and cope with change much better than either cardinal or fixed signs.

In fact your sign is probably the most prone to fluctuation, because you are a water sign and water is fluid. Water naturally takes the shape of its surrounding environment and so do you. It's critical therefore to surround yourself with positive energy and worthwhile people, for you are easily influenced by others.

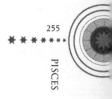

> *Other people simply don't have your depth of understanding. Mostly they find you difficult to fathom.*

Water flows in all directions. It can be deep or shallow, it might be still and clear like a mirror, or murky and muddy; either way it's difficult to see exactly what is going on beneath the surface.

Fish are the only creatures in the zodiac that live totally in a watery world and cannot breathe air. Other people simply don't have your depth of understanding. Mostly they find you difficult to fathom.

YOUR GODS AND MYTHS

More than any other sign you understand that myths and legends contain pearls of wisdom passed down through the generations. You love to immerse yourself in a good story and have such a vivid imagination you are good at creating your own stories too. The world truly needs your rich imagination. There are a host of mythological characters and gods linked to your sign.

Neptune—God of the sea

Neptune/Poseidon was the god of the sea. When the Olympian gods came to power, Zeus, Hades and Poseidon drew lots to see who would rule. Jupiter/Zeus took the sky and became supreme god, Pluto/Hades was granted the Underworld, and Neptune became ruler of the sea. They agreed between them to jointly govern the Earth.

Neptune lived in a golden castle on the ocean floor and rode the waves in a chariot drawn by sea-horses.

> *You love to immerse yourself in a good story and are good at creating your own stories too.*

By all accounts he was a very moody god and would sometimes strike the ground with his trident and cause earthquakes.

Because the planet Neptune was discovered relatively recently, the association with Pisces is a product of modern-day astrology. Nevertheless, it's appropriate that the god of the sea is linked with Pisces.

As god of the oceans, Neptune is a kind of vessel in which a host of water-dwelling creatures—including dolphins, mermaids, sea nymphs and sirens—reside, and all possess a mysterious mystical allure. Wherever water appears, you can be sure the magic of Pisces is present.

Jupiter—Supreme sky god

Before Neptune was discovered, Jupiter[1] was your only ruling planet. Jupiter rules Sagittarius too, so you have a few things in common with your Sagittarian cousins, in particular both signs are highly spiritual.

And like Sagittarians, you don't like having restrictions imposed upon you, but while they quickly take flight when they feel boxed in, you are a more slippery customer. Your strategy is to evade and subtly elude capture.

On the whole you are unaware of limitations. As far as you are concerned, everything is somehow invisibly connected, there are no discernable boundaries. You have such a universal perspective it's hard for you to see any difference between what is real and what is imagined.

The other thing you share with Sagittarians is the belief that if something is good then more of it must be better. This is another reason why overindulgence is such an easy trap for you. Like goldfish that keep eating whatever is there to be eaten, you often don't realise when you have reached your limits.

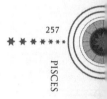

Dionysus—God of wine, nature and ecstasy

Dionysus was also known by his Roman name, Bacchus. He was the god of wine, ecstasy and nature. His followers would dance and drink themselves into a frenzied trance-like rapture.

Dionysus could change himself into a variety of creatures. You too are a chameleon, who can effortlessly adapt to your surroundings. You wear many different masks, so it can be difficult for others to know who you really are. Even you don't really know.

These days many people turn to drugs in order to experience an altered state of consciousness. When reality comes flooding in and you lose your sense of enchantment, you might be tempted to turn to drugs or alcohol to escape.

But drugs have side-effects and your sign is especially sensitive to chemicals. There are much more creative ways to be uplifted. Music, poetry and art are far better options. Religious devotion and falling in love are other ways to have an ecstatic experience. The word 'ecstasy' means to stand outside oneself. More than any other sign you have the natural ability to do this.

You carry a feeling of magical enchantment within you. You really don't need alcohol or drugs to transcend reality.

Nature too provides you with a feeling of spiritual wellbeing and for this reason it's important for you to regularly spend time in the natural environment where your soul feels at peace.

WHAT YOUR PLANETS REVEAL ABOUT YOU

The planet Neptune is aptly named, for it's a beautiful deep blue just like the mysterious ocean depths. Blue is a calming colour, naturally associated with water. It's serene, tranquil and soothing. These qualities are also found in your soul.

Neptune was discovered in 1846, but it was almost found much earlier. In 1612, Galileo, who was himself a Pisces, sighted Neptune though his telescope, but mistook it for a fixed star, so the elusive planet lived up to its reputation. At that time, Neptune was making a conjunction to Jupiter, your other ruling planet.

Neptune moves around the Sun in an orbit of 165 years, spending thirteen years in each sign of the zodiac. 2009 is the 165-year anniversary of Neptune's discovery and also a year when Jupiter and Neptune align. Having been through one full cycle of Neptune since it was discovered, we could say that the human race is crossing a threshold into a new era of spiritual awareness. We are beginning to awaken to the interconnectedness of everything, potentially leading us towards a truly universal understanding.

Located at the outer reaches of our solar system, Neptune can't be seen without the aid of a telescope. It's a long way from the Earth, around four light-hours in fact, compared to only eight light-minutes from the Earth to the Sun.

Because Neptune is so distant, you feel removed from earthly reality. Yet somehow Neptune is strangely reminiscent of the Earth, for it is the only other 'blue' planet.

Because Neptune is so distant, you also feel remote from earthly reality and yet Neptune is strangely reminiscent of the Earth, for it is the only other 'blue' planet.

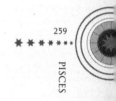

WHAT MAKES YOU TICK?

We all start out in life completely unconscious. Before we are born we float in a restful liquid world inside our mother's womb. When the time comes, we are rudely awakened and thrust into this world where we must learn to fend for ourselves.

As a Pisces, there is a large part of you that longs to return to the safety and magic of this pre-conscious state. In many ways, you never quite leave it.

Pisces people often have psychic experiences. Perhaps you see auras, or ghosts, or maybe you have prophetic dreams.

The unconscious is infinite and universal. You understand the depth and importance of this unseen world filled with dreams, symbols and images.

Children live in a magical world of fantasy. We all spend the first few years of life without any conscious awareness, but gradually we awaken. Our consciousness grows as we learn about ourselves and the world around us.

You retain the wonder and magic of childhood.
Fairytales and make-believe are just as real to you
as sandcastles.

Somehow you manage to retain the wonder and magic of childhood. Fairytales and make-believe are just as real to you as sandcastles.

Many people with Pisces emphasised in their birth charts have a great talent for music or art that is often seen early in life.

Interestingly, quite a number of Pisceans also excel at maths and physics, like Albert Einstein. Maybe this has something to do with the fact that the universe and everything in it can be understood in terms of mathematical equations.

Aquarius is the sign before Pisces, so you intrinsically understand the most complicated scientific concepts without necessarily having studied them. In particular, you seem to be able to comprehend theories used to explain and describe life itself.

Not that you are the least bit interested in facts, figures or logic for their own sake. What really matters to you is the spiritual dimension. You know beyond a doubt there is meaning and intelligence within all creation.

You may have noticed there's a spiral pattern common to the structure of both galaxies and DNA. As above; so below. Perhaps you first became aware of this when you were at the beach one day collecting seashells, and noticed they too have the same spiral pattern.

These naturally occurring spirals contain a magical, yet simple, mathematical formula, known as the Golden Ratio, which is intrinsic to life itself.[2] It's a natural pattern of growth.

Many Pisceans are passionate about surfing or fishing
or feel it's essential to live close to water, the source
of all life.

In spiritual terms, the spiral symbolises our journey towards enlightenment.

Whether your beliefs are aligned to traditional religious teachings, or something more spiritually modern, having something to believe in is essential to your wellbeing.

It's quite normal for Pisceans to have psychic experiences. Perhaps you see auras, or ghosts, or maybe you have prophetic dreams.

At first these experiences might have been quite scary. Or maybe you assumed that everyone was equally attuned to these vibrations, only to discover most people tend to dismiss such things as rubbish, or think you are completely crazy—or both.

There are many mysteries in this world and beyond. While more rational signs tend to dismiss crop circles, UFOs and meaningful synchronicity as the products of a deluded mind, or mere coincidence, you accept and believe.

As far as you're concerned, there's no right or wrong, no black or white. Everything is in shades of blue, all is connected.

The rational view of the world is that everything is separate from everything else. For a long time scientists have been trying to isolate everything in the world into individual components in order to study them objectively. But now they are starting to catch on. Objectivity is an illusion. Quantum theory has made them think again. It's a paradox to them, but not to you.

261
✱ ✱ ✱ ✱ ✱ ✱ ✱

PISCES

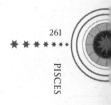

As far as you're concerned, there's no right or wrong,
no black or white. Everything is in shades of blue,
all is connected.

You have no difficulty whatsoever accepting the unseen and the mysterious; it's the real world that gets in the way and causes you problems. You can occasionally become disillusioned.

It's times like these when you like to go to the beach. Many Pisceans are passionate about surfing or fishing or feel it's essential to live close to water, the source of all life.

Dreams, images, moods and impressions are the language of the unconscious; this is the language you speak. The unconscious mind is where our memories are stored too, which is why Pisces people are able to recall the past—even past lives—with such clarity.

Each impression is captured by your mind like a photograph. In fact photography is one of many creative pursuits where your artistic gifts can find an outlet.

The universal language of music is another way to record and express impressions and feelings. Film-making and acting are another branch of the arts where Pisceans often excel.

The arts are a natural career choice but you are equally happy working near water, or with plants or animals. Your natural sympathy makes you a gifted healer and counsellor too.

My grandfather was a Pisces and an artist. A true bohemian, he was also a great storyteller and something of a philosopher. When he was young he used to drink like a fish and was swept up into the wild Dionysian never-ending party that was 1920s Sydney.

He once told me how he gave up smoking and drinking. One day he was trying to focus on a piece of artwork, and he would have a drink and a cigarette, to help him concentrate. Then he'd have another, and another, and nothing would ever get done. He became so annoyed with himself and his endless procrastination that around the age of 40 he gave up drinking and smoking, just like that. He just threw the cigarettes away and never had another drink.

Ultimately it's about believing in yourself.

Right throughout his life until the age of 92, he kept painting, drawing, sculpting and writing. He fought and won the struggle with his downstream fish. He learned that in the end it's just a question of taking action.

American Edgar Cayce was a gifted psychic who devoted his life to helping others. Known as 'The Sleeping Prophet', Cayce would enter a trance state in which his spirit would leave his body and visit people all over the world in order to diagnose their medical conditions and prescribe treatment. He helped to cure thousands of people. Cayce established the Association for Research and Enlightenment, which today houses a catalogue of his many readings and continues his work.

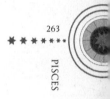

This is the main problem that Pisceans face. If it's not escaping via alcohol, it's something else that causes the distraction. There are just so many possibilities in life, you can end up swimming around in circles, getting nowhere. Then, just when you are set on a particular course, that 'other fish' jumps into your boat and starts flapping about; you never know whether to take it on board, or let it live to fight another day.

Going with the flow might feel right, but if you follow the fish downstream you'll never reach your spawning grounds where creative opportunity awaits. If you believed more in yourself, you'd know which way to swim.

Over time you'll discover how to have more faith in yourself and develop a stronger sense of identity, for the sign that follows Pisces is Aries, the sign at the very beginning of the zodiac, and this is where you are heading.

The end of Pisces is the beginning of Aries where the spiral zodiac has turned a full 360 degrees. Though you contain a little bit of every other sign, ultimately its about believing in yourself.

THE REALLY IMPORTANT
THINGS IN YOUR LIFE

Universal love

*Your deep compassion makes you feel somehow
spiritually responsible for the suffering of others.*

SECRETS OF THE ZODIAC

You accept that everyone is on their own unique journey. It doesn't bother you one iota what others think of you, but even so you probably don't share your innermost secrets very often. What you are really looking for is a special connection with someone you feel will understand and accept you. One of the most rapturous feelings we ever experience is falling in love. When we fall in love we enter a world that is not quite real. We lose ourselves and feel a heightened state of ecstasy and joy. The world looks wonderful and full of miraculous possibilities.

More than any other sign, you love to be in love, for this is one way you can escape the everyday world and transcend reality. You'll sacrifice anything and everything for love.

Life can feel shallow and dry when romance is missing, so you're eager to take the plunge; so keen in fact that sometimes you dive in too quickly and find yourself hooked up with the wrong person.

It's truly commendable that you never really lose your sense of wonder, but at the same time you are so acutely sensitive; a kind of psychic sponge, absorbing the moods and feelings of others. When people or animals are suffering, you feel it too.

*When you give unselfishly to others, you feel a deep
sense of spiritual reward.*

Your deep compassion can make you feel somehow spiritually responsible for the suffering of others and you're always at the ready to give a helping hand when anyone is in need.

When you give unselfishly to others, you feel a deep sense of spiritual reward, but you run the risk of losing your identity in the process, for you often just give too much. This is something you need to guard against.

You are so acutely sensitive, a kind of psychic sponge,
absorbing the moods and feelings of others. When
people or animals are suffering, you feel it too.

The two fish that symbolise Pisces are thought to be Venus and Cupid (Aphrodite and Eros) who, when escaping from the monster Typhon, tied themselves together with a cord of love before plunging into the sea and turning into fish. Likewise, there are times when you need to escape the harsh realities of the world. Love makes your spirit soar and overflow with joy. It is then that you know you are part of something magical and truly universal.

SHARING YOUR KNOWLEDGE

How you get along with others

People you can teach:	Air signs—Gemini, Libra, Aquarius
Compatible similar signs:	Water signs—Cancer, Scorpio, Pisces
Compatible complementary signs:	Earth signs—Taurus, Virgo, Capricorn
People you can learn from:	Fire signs—Aries, Leo, Sagittarius

Relating to air signs (Gemini, Libra, Aquarius)

Air signs are clever at managing everyday reality, but they have no idea about feelings. They live in their heads and have trouble seeing beneath the surface of things. You, on the other hand, are in touch with your instincts and emotions, easily understand subtle nuances, but have trouble logically reasoning things out and dealing with the real world. Air and water are poles apart, so any relationship between these elements is especially difficult.

To make matters worse, air signs are often critical of water signs. Air thinks water is slow and dense, so you tend to feel inferior when air signs are around.

Because the water element follows the air element, you can actually teach air signs a thing or two. They think they have all the answers, but actually they don't.

The good news is that because the water element follows the air element, you can actually teach air signs a thing or two. They think they have all the answers, but actually they don't.

Neptune's orbit is twice as long as that of Uranus, the ruling planet of Aquarius, so you can make even the most highly evolved Aquarian stop and think twice.

Air signs are sceptical about your instinctual way of relating to the world, but a time eventually comes when they notice that you actually know things they don't, and then they will want to know why you didn't tell them.

Air signs are generally afraid of emotions and feelings and are sceptical about anything psychic or spiritual. The deep waters of the unconscious are literally terrifying to air signs, because these things are not 'rational'.

Despite the many differences between you, there are some areas where air and water can find common ground.

Neptune's orbit is twice as long as that of Uranus, the ruling planet of Aquarius, so you can make even the most highly evolved Aquarian stop and think twice.

Geminis are mutable and changeable, like you; it's just that they live in their heads rather than their hearts. You share some similar characteristics with Librans too, for they are lovers of art, are keen to maintain peace and harmony, and will also make great sacrifices for the sake of others—just like you. You also understand why Aquarians are interested in the future of humanity, but you possess a much deeper and broader vision.

Relating to water signs (Cancer, Scorpio, Pisces)

All water signs are sensitive, emotional people who feel things deeply. You can always find emotional support and a safe haven with other water signs. Most of the time water/water relationships are mutually supportive, but sometimes you can take each other on a downward spiral.

When one water sign is going through a down period, the other will automatically feel sympathy and also begin to feel down. But when you are up, they are up too.

When you are looking for emotional support, your fellow water signs will provide it.

Relationships with Cancerians are highly creative and lots of fun. Scorpios can help you develop some staying power. Other Pisceans will, of course, understand you better than anyone, but the positives and negatives of this relationship will be amplified.

Relating to earth signs (Taurus, Virgo, Capricorn)

Water and earth are naturally compatible for earth signs provide the form and structure you need. They have practical skills which can help you turn your beautiful dreams into a tangible living reality.

Earth signs bring stability into your life, and they are good with money too.

Sometimes you find them rather dull and ordinary, but you infuse imagination and emotion into their otherwise black and white, humdrum existence, so they benefit too.

Earth signs bring stability to your life.

Capricorn is probably your most compatible sign, for Capricorns are really fish-tailed goats; Taurus is also a good match for you for they are romantic souls who appreciate love, beauty and art.

Virgo is your opposite sign and, as with all pairs of opposites, there is often a magnetic attraction. But the Virgo/Pisces relationship can be fraught with problems, because opposite signs often bring out the worst in each other.

Although in some ways you are compatible, and can learn a great deal about yourself from this relationship, opposite signs tend to unconsciously project all the unwanted aspects of their personalities onto each other, so this relationship can go down the gurgler pretty fast. But in highly evolved souls, a relationship between opposites can be one of the most romantic, beautiful and joyous of life's experiences.

Relating to fire signs (Aries, Leo, Sagittarius)

Fire sign people will stress you out because they push you to do things. They want you to be more dynamic, extroverted and outgoing. You will probably try to slip through their net, but you can nevertheless learn a great deal from them.

When it comes to courage, taking the initiative and acting independently, you know you struggle.

Fire signs see when you are floundering and can point the way forward. They're there to help you become more assertive and courageous, and encourage you to express yourself with more self-confidence.

WHAT YOU NEED TO LEARN

To believe in yourself

It really would be fantastic if you could wave a magic wand and change the whole world into a heavenly paradise, but in the meantime you need to work out a way to manage the reality of daily life.

You'd prefer to live in your dreams rather than in the real world. It's better to avoid problems and confrontation and live in peace, isn't it? You're just so sensitive that facing the outside world is really daunting. When reality comes flooding in, it can overwhelm you. But if you continually avoid life you can easily waste it all, and life, as the saying goes, is for living.

The more you avoid taking action, the more difficult it becomes to find the courage to do so. More than anything you need to develop a stronger ego and in order to do that, you first need to believe in yourself.

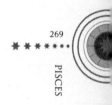

When you start to believe in yourself, you find your inner inspiration, the spark of creative impulse that fires both your imagination and your courage.

You truly are incredibly gifted and creative, but in order to create you must actually DO things.

When you start to believe in yourself, you connect with your inner inspiration, that spark of creative impulse that fires your imagination and enthusiasm.

TAKING THE NEXT STEP

A good place to start is to develop your relationships with fire signs. They are highly creative and imaginative people, just like you; but unlike you, they're naturally outgoing and confident. They have powerful egos and believe in themselves. Better yet, they are keen to encourage you to develop some of these traits.

Just like you want to help the air signs develop more compassion and an inner spiritual life, fire signs want to help you develop the life skills you lack, such as assertiveness and self-confidence.

You actually have a great deal in common with fire signs, although you probably don't see it that way.

Aries people are in touch with their emotions; Leos are highly creative and generous; while spirituality and meaning are important to Sagittarians.

But you tend to see fire signs as aggressive, too full-on, too focused on themselves, too driven, just 'too' everything. When you feel this way, it's a sure sign you should try to take their advice.

Aries, the sign that follows Pisces, is the first sign of the zodiac, which might seem like it's a long way away from where you are right now, but it really isn't that far at all. It just requires a leap of faith on your part, and faith is something you have plenty of.

Fire signs possess the leadership qualities you lack. Obviously you are a water sign, not a fire sign, so you are never going to be like them, nor should you. But now and then it wouldn't hurt you to take a leaf out of their book.

Aries, the sign that follows Pisces, is the first sign of the zodiac, which might seem like it's a long way away from where you are right now, but it really isn't that far at all.

When you combine Neptune's beautiful deep blue colour with the dynamic red of Mars/Aries, you create violet, the colour at the end of the rainbow, that magical place where dreams come true.

TIPS FOR PISCES

- ⯎ Believe in yourself.
- ⯎ As your imagination inspires you, create, create, create.
- ⯎ When you're distracted or daydreaming, channel this into new projects.
- ⯎ Now and then pinch yourself so you know you're a real person.
- ⯎ Learn to have as much compassion for yourself as you do for others.
- ⯎ Don't escape into drugs or alcohol—spiral up, not down.
- ⯎ Consider the advice of the fire signs you meet.

YOUR GIFT TO THE WORLD

How you can make a real difference

Your special gift to the world is your depth of imagination and understanding of the unconscious. If the world were populated only by Pisceans, we would all live in a world of universal peace and understanding, an idyllic paradise overflowing with beauty, music, romance and the bounty of nature.

While it's true that you do need to learn to be more assertive, your true gift is to guide others towards a deeper spiritual understanding.

FAMOUS PERSONALITIES WITH THE SUN IN PISCES INCLUDE:

Douglas Adams

Robert Altman

Meher Baba

Drew Barrymore

Alexander Graham Bell

Peter Brock

Edgar Cayce

Frederic Chopin

Kurt Cobain

Nicholas Copernicus

Albert Einstein

Galileo

Mikhail Gorbachev

George Harrison

Jennifer Love Hewitt

L. Ron Hubbard

Victor Hugo

Michelangelo

Rudolph Nureyev

Auguste Renoir

Rudolph Steiner

Sharon Stone

Elizabeth Taylor

Antonio Vivaldi

NOTES

Introduction

1 It's quite possible that astrology began much earlier; however, the oldest written records pertaining to astrology found to date are from this era and region of the Middle East. Rob Hand's account of the origins of astrology can be found at <http://www.astro.com/people/hand_his_e.htm> [20 July 2008]. *The Dawn of Astrology: A cultural history of western astrology* by Nick Campion, Continuum, UK, USA, 2008, gives a detailed historic account of the development of astrology through the ages

2 Fred Gettings, *The Arkana Dictionary of Astrology*, Penguin Books, London, UK, 1990, p. 562. This concept is known as the Zodiac of Life, or Zodiacus Vitae. During the time of Shakespeare, a book by Marcellus Palingenius Stellatus called *Zodiacus Vitae* was a standard text in English schools and was widely published in other parts of Europe. First published circa 1531, it was reprinted many times until at least 1722. Marcellus Palingenius Stellatus and Foster Watson, *The Zodiacus Vitae of Marcellus Palingenius Stellatus*, Philip Wellby, London, 1908

3 C.G. Jung, *Memories, Dreams, Reflections*, Fontana paperbacks, London, 1983, pp. 342–3

Aries

1 When referring to the seasons, the northern hemisphere is used throughout this book

2 NASA <http://spaceflight.nasa.gov/gallery/images/mars/meteorites/html/s94_032549.html> [30 November 2007]

Taurus

1   See Capricorn and Aquarius notes

2   The Golden Ratio is found everywhere in nature in naturally occuring spirals, such as in shells, just as Venus stands on a shell in the famous painting of her birth, by Botticelli. See also Pisces notes

3   NASA <http://solarsystem.nasa.gov/planetselector.cfm?Object=Venus> [30 November 2007]

4   History paints Lucrezia Borgia as a murderous femme fatale, but it's equally, if not more plausible, that she was used as a pawn by her father, Pope Alexander VI, to further his own political interests

Gemini

1   See Virgo notes

Cancer

1   See Virgo notes

2   NASA <http://history.nasa.gov/ap11ann/timelines.htm> [23 March 2008]

Leo

1   Apollo took the place of Helios, who was the original Sun god

Virgo

1   See Cancer notes

2   See Gemini notes

3   Demetra George, *Asteroid Goddesses*, ACS Publications, San Diego, 1986, p. 123

4   The purpose of the Dawn Mission is to study the solar system's earliest epoch by investigating Ceres and Vesta, two of the largest protoplanets that have remained intact since their formation. A protoplanet is a 'baby' planet whose growth was interrupted by the formation of Jupiter. Ceres and Vesta are clustered with many asteroids forming a

'belt' between Mars and Jupiter. Ceres is thought to be primitive and wet, while Vesta is more evolved and dry, which is in keeping with their archetypal meaning <http://www.itnews.com.au/newsstory.aspx?ClaNID=21444> [2 June 2006]

5   See Gemini notes

Libra

1   See Taurus notes
2   See Taurus notes

Scorpio

1   Online Etymology Dictionary <http://www.etymonline.com/index.php?search=devil&searchmode=none> [15 June 2007]
2   See Virgo and Cancer notes
3   See Aries notes
4   NASA <http://www.nasa.gov/mission_pages/newhorizons/main/index.html> [17 July 2007]

Sagittarius

1   <http://solarsystem.nasa.gov/planets/profile.cfm?Object=Jupiter> [21 July 2007]
2   Albert Bigelow Pain, *Mark Twain, a Biography*, University of Adelaide, Electronic Texts Collection <http://etext.library.adelaide.edu.au/t/twain/mark/paine/appendix1.html> [15 July 2007]
3   ibid.
4   This saying has been variously attributed to James Dean, Jim Morrison and John Belushi, but appears to have originated from a 1947 novel, *Knock on Any Door*, by William Motley. Ames, Bob, 2004 quotes Tallet, Dennis <http://www.mindspring.com/~boba4-a/Oftquote.htm#LIVEFAST> [13 July 2007]

Capricorn

1   The Roman equivalent of these Greek gods and goddesses are Vesta, Ceres, Juno, Pluto, Neptune and Jupiter respectively

2   The term 'scapegoat' comes from the Hebrew custom of Yom Kippur, when a goat carried the sins of the people, freeing them from the consequences of sin. In Christian tradition the scapegoat is associated with Christ's suffering. Jack Tresidder, *1001 Symbols*, Duncan Baird Publishers, London, 2003, pp. 365–6

3   Geoffrey Cornelius, *The Complete Guide to the Constellations*, Duncan Baird Publishers, London, 2005, p. 57

Aquarius

1   See Capricorn notes

2   ibid.

3   Roy Willis, *World Mythology*, Duncan Baird Publishers, London, 1993, p. 130

4   See Capricorn notes

5   See Introduction notes

Pisces

1   See Sagittarius notes

    NASA <http://www.nasa.gov/worldbook/neptune_worldbook.html> [13 Jan 2008]

2   The Golden Ratio is based on a series of numbers known as the Fibonacci sequence of numbers; 1, 1, 2, 3, 5, 8, 13, 21, 34, 55, etc.—where the next number in the sequence is the sum of the earlier two. The ratio between each number is 1.618, known as the Golden Ratio. Geometrically, this sequence forms a perfect spiral that is intrinsic to nature, and can be seen in plants, shells and even DNA. For more information on this fascinating subject, just go fishing on the web. A good place to start is Dawson Merrill's Fib-Phi Link Page <http://www.goldenratio.org/info/> [1 Dec 2007]. See also Taurus notes

BIBLIOGRAPHY

Bolen, Jean Shinoda, *Goddesses in Everywoman*, HarperCollins Publishers, New York, 1984

——*Gods in Everyman*, HarperCollins Publishers, New York, 1989

Brau, Jean-Louis, Weaver, Helen and Edmands, Allan, *Larousse Encyclopedia of Astrology*, McGraw Hill Book Company, New York, 1977

Cornelius, Geoffrey, *The Complete Guide to the Constellations*, Duncan Baird Publishers, London, 2005

Cotterell, Arthur, *Classical Mythology*, Lorenz Books, New York, 2002

Davison, Ronald, C., *Astrology*, Acro Publications, Great Britain, 1969

George, Demetra, *Asteroid Goddesses*, ACS Publications, San Diego, 1986

Gettings, Fred, *The Arkana Dictionary of Astrology*, Penguin Books, London, 1990

Goldschneider, Gary and Elffers, Joost, *The Secret Language of Birthdays*, Penguin Group, New York, 1994

Graves, Robert, *The Greek Myths: 1*, Penguin Books, London, 1955

Greene, Liz, *Relating; An Astrological Guide to Living with Others on a Small Planet*, Samuel Weiser, Inc., York Beach, Maine, 1978

——*Neptune and the Quest for Redemption*, Samuel Weiser, Inc., York Beach, Maine, 1996

Greene, Liz and Sharman-Burke, Juliet, *The Mythic Journey*, Simon and Schuster, East Roseville, Australia, 1999

Howell, Alice, O., *Jungian Symbolism in Astrology*, Theological Publishing House, Wheaton, UK, 1987

Johnson, Robert, A., *Ecstasy*, HarperCollins Publishers, San Francisco, 1989

——*She*, HarperCollins Publishers, New York, 1989

Jung, C.G., *Memories, Dreams, Reflections*, Fontana Paperbacks, London, 1983

Pearsall, Judy and Trumble, Bill (editors), *The Oxford English Reference Dictionary*, Oxford University Press, Oxford, UK, 2003

Pinsent, John, *Greek Mythology*, Hamlyn Publishing Group Ltd, London, 1982

Sobel, Dava, *The Planets*, HarperCollins Publishers, London, 2006

Sullivan, Erin, *Retrograde Planets*, Samuel Weiser, Inc., York Beach, Maine, 2000

Tresidder, Jack, *1001 Symbols*, Duncan Baird Publishers, London, 2003

Willis, Roy (editor), *World Mythology*, Duncan Baird Publishers, London, 1993

Web sources

Astrotheme <http://www.astrotheme.fr/en/portraits/W.htm>

Encyclopedia Mythica <http://www.pantheon.org>

Great-Quotes.com <http://www.great-quotes.com>

Online Etymology Dictionary <http://www.etymonline.com>

Theoi Greek Mythology <http://www.theoi.com>

Digital Book Index Aesop's Fables <http://digitalbookindex.com/_search/search010child03t.asp>

Aesopica: Aesop's Fables in English, Latin and Greek <http://www.mythfolklore.net/aesopica/caxton/33.htm>